Newmark LEARNING™
5

STAAR
Reading
Warm-Ups
& Test Practice

ALIGNED TO THE
TEXAS STAAR EXAM

Newmark Learning
145 Huguenot Street • New Rochelle, NY • 10801

Editor: Jessica Pippin
Designer: Raquel Hernández
Illustrator: Brandon Fall

ISBN: 978-1-4788-0741-4

Table of Contents

Contents	Page

Introduction

STAAR Reading Warm-Ups & Test Practice is designed to prepare students for the STAAR Reading Tests. The STAAR Reading Assessments, administered every spring to students in Grades 3–8, assess students' ability to:

- Use text evidence to support ideas about texts
- Develop analytical skills in multiple text genres
- Use reading strategies to support making meaning from text
- Understand academic vocabulary

The goal of the STAAR Reading Tests is for students to read and understand a variety of literary and informational texts. In the reading exams, greater emphasis will be placed on critical analysis rather than literal understanding of texts.

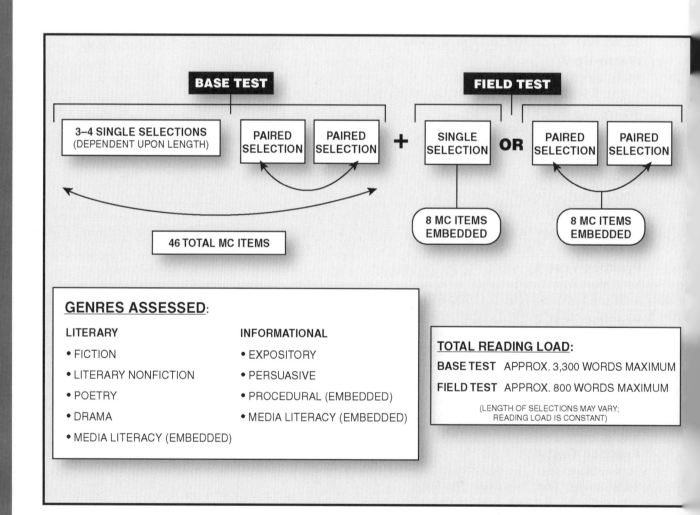

BASE TEST

3–4 SINGLE SELECTIONS (DEPENDENT UPON LENGTH)

PAIRED SELECTION **PAIRED SELECTION**

46 TOTAL MC ITEMS

+

FIELD TEST

SINGLE SELECTION **OR** **PAIRED SELECTION** **PAIRED SELECTION**

8 MC ITEMS EMBEDDED   **8 MC ITEMS EMBEDDED**

GENRES ASSESSED:

LITERARY
- FICTION
- LITERARY NONFICTION
- POETRY
- DRAMA
- MEDIA LITERACY (EMBEDDED)

INFORMATIONAL
- EXPOSITORY
- PERSUASIVE
- PROCEDURAL (EMBEDDED)
- MEDIA LITERACY (EMBEDDED)

TOTAL READING LOAD:

BASE TEST APPROX. 3,300 WORDS MAXIMUM

FIELD TEST APPROX. 800 WORDS MAXIMUM

(LENGTH OF SELECTIONS MAY VARY; READING LOAD IS CONSTANT)

Readiness & Supporting Standards

The STAAR tests assess students based on specific Texas Essential Knowledge and Skills (TEKS). For each grade, the Texas Education Agency (TEA) has identified a set of knowledge and skills drawn from the TEKS. This set of knowledge and skills is known as **readiness standards**. These skills will be assessed and emphasized on the STAAR tests. Readiness standards make up 60%–70% of the STAAR Reading Test.

According to the TEA, readiness standards have the following characteristics:

- They are essential for success in the current grade or course.
- They are important for preparedness for the next grade or course.
- They support college and career readiness.
- They necessitate in-depth instruction.
- They address broad and deep ideas.

The remaining set of knowledge and skills is known as **supporting standards**. According to the TEA, they have the following characteristics:

- Although introduced in the current grade or course, they may be emphasized in a subsequent year.
- Although reinforced in the current grade or course, they may be emphasized in a previous year.
- They play a role in preparing students for the next grade or course but not a central role.
- They address more narrowly defined ideas.

A skills chart is included on page 12 of *STAAR Reading Warm-Ups & Test Practice.* A correlation chart that indicates what skills are covered in each question is included on page 14.

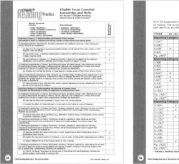 

How are the STAAR Reading Tests structured?

The STAAR Reading Tests include 40 multiple-choice questions. Students will read four or five selections and answer a set of questions after each selection. Beginning in Grade 4, students might compare two selections and answer questions.

Specific features of the STAAR Reading Test include the following:

- The tests will have a four-hour time limit.
- Tests will be administered in paper format.
- STAAR will focus on the most critical TEKS, which will better measure the academic performance of students from elementary to middle school and eventually high school.
- All questions will be multiple-choice.

Reporting Categories	Number of Standards		Number of Questions	
Reporting Category 1: **Understanding Across Genres**	Readiness Standards	2	**6**	
	Supporting Standards	1		
	Total	3		
Reporting Category 2: **Understanding/Analysis of** **Literary Texts**	Readiness Standards	4	**18**	
	Supporting Standards	8		
	Total	12		
Reporting Category 3: **Understanding/Analysis of** **Informational Texts**	Readiness Standards	6	**16**	
	Supporting Standards	2		
	Total	8		
Readiness Standards	**Total Number of Standards**	12	60%–70%	24–28
Supporting Standards	**Total Number of Standards**	11	30%–40%	12–16
Total Number of Questions on Test			**40**	

How will this book help students prepare?

STAAR Reading Warm-Ups & Test Practice is designed to help prepare students for the STAAR assessments. There are ten Warm-Ups and five Practice Tests.

Selections include every genre covered on the STAAR skills assessment. There is an assortment of literary and informational texts, including poetry and literary nonfiction. In the selections for Grade 5, the genres assessed are fiction, literary nonfiction, poetry, drama, media literacy, expository, persuasive, and procedural.

Tear-out answer keys for the Warm-Ups and Practice Tests are provided in the back, as well as sample bubble sheets for students to use while taking the tests.

Warm-Ups

STAAR Reading Warm-Ups & Test Practice includes ten Warm-Ups, which are short tests that are designed to provide students with an opportunity for quick, guided practice.

The ten Warm-Ups feature short reading selections that include examples of the genres that students are required to read in each grade level and will encounter on the test.

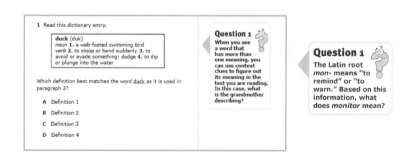

The Warm-Ups also include prompts with each question. These prompts are designed to guide students through the test. They model the thinking needed for answering questions, provide reading strategies, and include additional support for answering the questions. A variety of skills and standards are addressed in the Warm-Up prompts.

Practice Tests

The Practice Tests feature longer selections that match the selection lengths that will be used for the STAAR Assessments and the number of corresponding questions. These selections provide students with experience reading the longer and more complex texts they will have to read on the assessments.

Three of the Practice Tests also feature paired selections. Students are required to read paired selections in Grade 5. The Practice Tests are designed to be flexible. Students can take each test individually, or they can take a longer test featuring two selections and twice the number of questions.

The paired selections give students the opportunity to compare and contrast texts and integrate information from multiple texts, as required beginning in Grade 4.

Literature

Informational Texts

Paired Texts

Each selection is followed by a complete set of questions that reflect the number of questions students will find with each selection on the assessments. In addition, similar to the Warm-Ups, the Practice Tests also include the types of questions students will see on the assessments.

Questions with multiple answers

Tear-Out Answer Keys & Bubble Sheets

The answers to all the Warm-Ups and Practice Tests are provided in the Answer Key beginning on page 109. The Answer Key includes the standards correlations for each question.

Sample bubble sheets are provided on page 132. These bubble sheets resemble general answer sheets that students might use on a standardized test. They add to the authenticity of the test-taking experience and also allow students to practice filling out a bubble sheet.

Answer Key

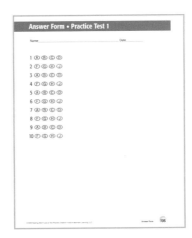

Answer Form

How to Use This Book

Warm-Ups

The Warm-Ups are designed to be quick and easy practice for students. They can be used in a variety of ways:

- Assign Warm-Ups for homework.

- Use them for quick review in class.

- Use them for targeted review of key standards. The correlation chart on page 14 can identify Warm-Ups that address the skills you want to focus on.

Practice Tests

The longer Practice Tests can be used to prepare students in the weeks before the assessments. They can also be used to assess students' reading comprehension throughout the year.

Test-Taking Experience

To simulate an actual STAAR Reading Test, choose two of the paired Practice Tests (15 questions each) and one of the single Practice Tests (10 questions each). This will create a 40-question test, which is how many questions are on the actual STAAR test. Use the sample bubble sheets in the back of the book, as well.

You may want to read the section below when introducing the test. This is similar to what is announced before each STAAR test.

Say: *Today you will be taking the reading test of the State of Texas Assessments of Academic Readiness, or STAAR. It is important for you to do your best. If you have any questions or need any help, please raise your hand.*

I cannot help answer any test questions. I will be able to help you only with questions about the directions. If you do not know the answer to a question, choose the answer you think might be correct. Remember that you may write in your test booklet if you would like to make notes.

You will now take the reading test by yourself. Remember to mark your answers very carefully and make your marks dark and neat. If there are no more questions, you may begin.

Test-Taking Tips

Below are some helpful test-taking tips for students to consider before the STAAR Reading Test is administered.

- Be well rested the day of the test. It is important to eat a balanced breakfast the morning of the test.

- Begin the morning of the test with a positive attitude and confidence. Try to remain relaxed throughout the test.

- Have all materials ready before the test begins: pencil, eraser, and any other required materials.

- Be aware of how the test is structured so there are no surprises when the exam begins.

- Manage time. Taking practice exams, such as the ones provided in *STAAR Reading Warm-Ups & Test Practice*, will help you learn how to pace yourself and complete all answers in the allotted time.

- STAAR Reading Assessments are all multiple-choice. Cross out incorrect answers and use the process of elimination to figure out the correct answer.

- Many of the answers can be found in the text. Go back to each passage and underline important parts.

- Fill in the answer sheet carefully, leaving no stray pencil marks.

- If finished early, go back through the test and check over the answers. It is never good to rush through an exam.

STAAR ★

Reading Warm-Ups & Test Practice

Eligible Texas Essential Knowledge and Skills
for Grade 5 STAAR Reading Warm-Ups & Test Practice

Genres Assessed:		Readiness Standard
Literary	**Informational**	
• Fiction (Readiness)	• Expository (Readiness)	
• Literary Nonfiction (Supporting)	• Persuasive (Supporting)	
• Poetry (Supporting)	• Procedural (Embedded)	
• Drama (Supporting	• Media Literacy (Embedded)	
• Media Literacy (Embedded)		
Reporting Category 1: Understanding and Analysis Across Genres Demonstrate an ability to understand and analyze a variety of written texts across reading genres.		
(2) Reading/Vocabulary Development. Students understand new vocabulary and use it when reading and writing. Students are expected to		
(A) determine the meaning of grade-level academic English words derived from Latin, Greek, or other linguistic roots and affixes;		✓
(B) use context (e.g., in-sentence restatement) to determine or clarify the meaning of unfamiliar or multiple meaning words;		✓
(E) use a dictionary, a glossary, or a thesaurus (printed or electronic) to determine the meanings, syllabication, pronunciations, alternate word choices, and parts of speech of words.		✓
(3) Reading/Comprehension of Literary Text/Theme and Genre. Students analyze, make inferences and draw conclusions about theme and genre in different cultural, historical, and contemporary contexts and provide evidence from the text to support their understanding. Students are expected to		
(A) compare and contrast the themes or moral lessons of several works of fiction from various cultures.		
(Figure 19) Reading/Comprehension Skills. Students use a flexible range of metacognitive reading skills in both assigned and independent reading to understand an author's message. Students will continue to apply earlier standards with greater depth in increasingly more complex texts as they become self-directed, critical readers. The student is expected to		
(F) make connections (e.g., thematic links, author analysis) between and across multiple texts of various genres and provide textual evidence.		✓
Reporting Category 2: Understanding and Analysis of Literary Texts The student will demonstrate an ability to understand and analyze literary texts.		
(3) Reading/Comprehension of Literary Text/Theme and Genre. Students analyze, make inferences and draw conclusions about theme and genre in different cultural, historical, and contemporary contexts and provide evidence from the text to support their understanding. Students are expected to		
(B) describe the phenomena explained in origin myths from various cultures;		
(C) explain the effect of a historical event or movement on the theme of a work of literature.		
(4) Reading/Comprehension of Literary Text/Poetry. Students understand, make inferences and draw conclusions about the structure and elements of poetry and provide evidence from text to support their understanding. Students are expected to		
(A) analyze how poets use sound effects (e.g., alliteration, internal rhyme, onomatopoeia, rhyme scheme) to reinforce meaning in poems.		
(5) Reading/Comprehension of Literary Text/Drama. Students understand, make inferences and draw conclusions about the structure and elements of drama and provide evidence from text to support their understanding.		
(6) Reading/Comprehension of Literary Text/Fiction. Students understand, make inferences and draw conclusions about the structure and elements of fiction and provide evidence from text to support their understanding. Students are expected to		
(A) describe incidents that advance the story or novel, explaining how each incident gives rise to or foreshadows future events;		✓
(B) explain the roles and functions of characters in various plots, including their relationships and conflicts;		✓
(C) explain different forms of third-person points of view in stories.		
(7) Reading/Comprehension of Literary Text/Literary Nonfiction. Students understand, make inferences and draw conclusions about the varied structural patterns and features of literary nonfiction and provide evidence from text to support their understanding. Students are expected to		
(A) identify the literary language and devices used in biographies and autobiographies, including how authors present major events in a person's life.		

(8) Reading/Comprehension of Literary Text/Sensory Language. Students understand, make inferences and draw conclusions about how an author's sensory language creates imagery in literary text and provide evidence from text to support their understanding. Students are expected to	
(A) evaluate the impact of sensory details, imagery, and figurative language in literary text.	✓
(14) Reading/Media Literacy. Students use comprehension skills to analyze how words, images, graphics, and sounds work together in various forms to impact meaning. Students continue to apply earlier standards with greater depth in increasingly more complex texts. Students are expected to	
(C) make inferences about text and use textual evidence to support understanding; Readiness Standard (Fiction) / Supporting Standard (Literary Nonfiction, Poetry, Drama)	
(Figure 19) Reading/Comprehension Skills. Students use a flexible range of metacognitive reading skills in both assigned and independent reading to understand an author's message. Students will continue to apply earlier standards with greater depth in increasingly more complex texts as they become self-directed, critical readers. The student is expected to	
(D) make inferences about text and use textual evidence to support understanding;	✓
(E) summarize and paraphrase texts in ways that maintain meaning and logical order within a text and across texts.	✓
Reporting Category 3: Understanding and Analysis of Informational Texts Demonstrate an ability to understand and analyze informational texts.	
(10) Reading/Comprehension of Informational Text/Culture and History. Students analyze, make inferences and draw conclusions about the author's purpose in cultural, historical, and contemporary contexts and provide evidence from the text to support their understanding. Students are expected to	
(A) summarize and paraphrase texts in ways that maintain meaning and logical order within a text and across texts.	
(11) Reading/Comprehension of Informational Text/Expository Text. Students analyze, make inferences and draw conclusions about expository text and provide evidence from text to support their understanding. Students are expected to	
(A) summarize the main ideas and supporting details in a text in ways that maintain meaning and logical order;	✓
(B) determine the facts in text and verify them through established methods;	
(C) analyze how the organizational pattern of a text (e.g., cause-and-effect, compare-and-contrast, sequential order, logical order, classification schemes) influences the relationships among the ideas;	✓
(D) use multiple text features and graphics to gain an overview of the contents of text and to locate information;	✓
(E) synthesize and make logical connections between ideas within a text and across two or three texts representing similar or different genres.	✓
(12) Reading/Comprehension of Informational Text/Persuasive Text. Students analyze, make inferences and draw conclusions about persuasive text and provide evidence from text to support their analysis. Students are expected to	
(A) identify the author's viewpoint or position and explain the basic relationships among ideas (e.g., parallelism, comparison, causality) in the argument;	
(B) recognize exaggerated, contradictory, or misleading statements in text.	
(13) Reading/Comprehension of Informational Text/Procedural Texts. Students understand how to glean and use information in procedural texts and documents. Students are expected to	
(A) interpret details from procedural text to complete a task, solve a problem, or perform procedures;	
(B) interpret factual or quantitative information presented in maps, charts, illustrations, graphs, timelines, tables, and diagrams.	
(14) Reading/Media Literacy. Students use comprehension skills to analyze how words, images, graphics, and sounds work together in various forms to impact meaning. Students continue to apply earlier standards with greater depth in increasingly more complex texts. Students are expected to	
(C) identify the point of view of media presentations.	
(Figure 19) Reading/Comprehension Skills. Students use a flexible range of metacognitive reading skills in both assigned and independent reading to understand an author's message. Students will continue to apply earlier standards with greater depth in increasingly more complex texts as they become self-directed, critical readers. The student is expected to	
(D) make inferences about text and use textual evidence to support understanding;	✓
(E) summarize and paraphrase texts in ways that maintain meaning and logical order within a text and across texts.	✓

All of the assessment items are correlated to the STAAR Standards for reading. The correlation chart below shows the standards that each Warm-Up and Practice Test addresses.

STAAR	W1	W2	W3	W4	W5	W6	W7	W8	W9	W10	PT1	PT2	PT3	PT4	PT5
Reporting Category 1															
5.2(A)*						✓		✓					✓	✓	
5.2(B)*			✓	✓					✓	✓		✓	✓		✓
5.2(E)*	✓										✓			✓	
5.3(A)			✓				✓						✓		
Fig. 19(F)*													✓	✓	
Reporting Category 2															
5.3(B)															✓
5.3(C)															✓
5.4(A)					✓										
5.6(A)*	✓						✓						✓		
5.6(B)*	✓		✓										✓		✓
5.6(C)	✓												✓		✓
5.7(A)										✓					
5.8(A)*					✓		✓						✓		✓
5.14(C)										✓				✓	✓
Fig. 19(D)*			✓		✓		✓		✓	✓		✓	✓		✓
Fig. 19(E)*					✓		✓						✓		✓
Reporting Category 3															
5.10(A)		✓		✓				✓				✓			
5.11(A)*		✓						✓			✓	✓		✓	
5.11(B)				✓							✓			✓	
5.11(C)*		✓		✓							✓			✓	
5.11(D)*						✓					✓				
5.11(E)*						✓					✓	✓		✓	
5.12(A)														✓	
5.12(B)														✓	
5.13(A)						✓									
5.13(B)						✓									
5.14(C)		✓						✓					✓		
Fig. 19(D)*											✓	✓			
Fig. 19(E)*											✓	✓		✓	

* indicates a Readiness Standard

Warm-Up ①

Read the selection and choose the best answer to each question.

STAAR
STATE OF TEXAS ASSESSMENTS OF ACADEMIC READINESS

5.2(E)
Use a dictionary, a glossary, or a thesaurus (printed or electronic) to determine the meanings, syllabication, pronunciations, alternate word choices, and parts of speech of words.

5.6(A)
Describe incidents that advance the story or novel, explaining how each incident gives rise to or foreshadows future events.

5.6(B)
Explain the roles and functions of characters in various plots, including their relationships and conflicts.

5.6(C)
Explain different forms of third-person points of view in stories.

Grandpa's Garden

1   Jayden pored over his grandma's old photo albums, struggling to remember his grandfather. There he was, holding Jayden on his lap, a gigantic grin on his face. Everything was gigantic about Grandpa, Jayden recollected—his hands, his feet, his laugh.

2   "Grandma," Jayden questioned, "how tall was Grandpa?"

3   "Oh, about six and a half feet, I reckon. Not as tall as those basketball players you like to watch, but tall enough to <u>duck</u> through the front door!" she chuckled.

4   "Maybe I'll get that tall," Jayden mused.

5   As he turned his attention back to the album, he noticed a series of cryptic photos of fruits and vegetables growing in a garden. There were tomatoes, strawberries, yellow squash, green beans—and, in one snapshot, Jayden's grandpa was hoisting a spotted green watermelon high overhead.

continued ➡

6   "No way Grandpa grew that watermelon!" exclaimed Jayden.

7   "Oh, yes, he did," retorted his grandma. "Your granddaddy definitely had a green thumb. He would dig and dig, turning the soil over until it was nice and soft. Then came planting time, and he set all those seeds in the ground by hand. Every day he watered, hoed, pulled weeds, and tended that garden."

8   "Where was it?" quizzed Jayden.

9   "Right yonder over there." She motioned with her head to the far side of the backyard.

10   "I don't see any garden," objected Jayden. "All I see is dirt and grass."

11   "Yes, well, there is nobody around to tend the garden anymore . . ." His grandma's voice trailed off. "How about you do it?" she said brightly.

12   "Sounds like a lot of work." Jayden didn't mean to speak that out loud, for he knew his grandmother would be disappointed by his attitude. "All right," he said resolutely. "I'll do it. Where do I start?"

13   "I'll turn on the hose and get the hoe!" Grandma said, exuberant.

Name_____ Date_____

1 Read this dictionary entry.

> **duck** \duk\
> *noun* **1.** a web-footed swimming bird
> *verb* **2.** to stoop or bend suddenly **3.** to
> avoid or evade something; to dodge **4.** to
> dip or plunge into the water

Which definition best matches the word <u>duck</u> as it is used in paragraph 3?

A Definition 1

B Definition 2

C Definition 3

D Definition 4

Question 1
When you see a word that has more than one meaning, you can use context clues to figure out its meaning in the text you are reading. In this case, what is the grandmother describing?

2 How does Jayden become interested in gardening?

F by watching basketball players on TV

G by reading a book about growing watermelons

H by finding an old garden plot in the backyard

J by looking at photos of his grandfather

Question 2
Reread paragraphs 1-4. What is Jayden doing at the beginning of the selection that causes him to become interested in gardening?

continued

Name_____ Date_____

Question 3

Dialogue can show what characters are thinking and feeling. Reread the answer choices, paying close attention to word choice. Which option shows Grandma's happiness at Jayden wanting to garden?

3 Which sentence from the story best shows that Grandma is pleased about Jayden starting to garden?

A *"Your granddaddy definitely had a green thumb."*

B *"Every day he watered, hoed, pulled weeds, and tended the garden."*

C *"How about you do it?" she said brightly.*

D *"I'll turn on the hose and get the hoe!" Grandma said, exuberant.*

Question 4

Look for clues about the narrator throughout the story. Think about who is telling the story. Is it an outside observer or one of the main characters? Pay attention to pronoun use in the selection.

4 Who is the narrator of this story?

F an outside observer

G Jayden

H Grandma

J Grandpa

Warm-Up ❷

Read the selection and choose the best answer to each question.

STAAR
STATE OF TEXAS ASSESSMENTS OF ACADEMIC READINESS

5.10(A)
Draw conclusions from the information presented by an author and evaluate how well the author's purpose was achieved.

5.11(A)
Summarize the main ideas and supporting details in a text in ways that maintain meaning and logical order.

5.11(C)
Analyze how the organizational pattern of a text influences the relationships among the ideas.

5.14(C)
Identify the point of view of media presentations.

Meet Sue

1   On August 12, 1990, a young woman by the name of Susan Hendrickson made a remarkable discovery. Located near the base of a cliff in South Dakota were the fossil remains of a dinosaur. But this was not just any dinosaur. It was a *Tyrannosaurus rex*, the "Tyrant Lizard King." The dinosaur had lain buried for almost 65 million years. As scientists worked to free the fossil from its resting place, they began to understand their amazing find. When fully uncovered, the dinosaur was almost 90 percent complete.

2   In 1997, the dinosaur's bones were put up for auction. In a little over eight minutes, the winning bid was made by the Field Museum of Chicago. The museum offered more than $8 million, the largest amount of money ever paid for a fossil. Now the dinosaur had both a home and a purpose.

continued ▶

3   "Sue," named after her discoverer, is considered to be the largest and best-preserved fossil of her kind. She is also the most complete, measuring 42 feet long from snout to tail and standing almost 13 feet tall. Sue weighs an incredible 3,922 pounds; the skull alone weighs 600 pounds. Of the 324 known bones that made a *T. rex*'s skeleton, Sue has a total of 224. In fact, Sue's body is so well preserved that scientists are actually able to see where the dinosaur's muscles were located, particularly in the tail area.

4   The *T. rex* was one of the last dinosaur species to live in North America, more than 67 million years ago. Because Sue is the most complete dinosaur fossil ever unearthed, she has tremendous value for people who study dinosaurs.

5   Sue continues to be the subject of great fascination among dinosaur lovers all over the world. And with Sue's help, we continue to learn more about these amazing creatures.

Name_____ Date_____

1 What is the main idea of this selection?

A The discovery of a *Tyrannosaurus rex* skeleton in 1990 was a valuable find for scientists.

B The *Tyrannosaurus rex* skeleton found in 1990 was bought for $8 million by a museum in Chicago.

C The *Tyrannosaurus rex* lived in North America more than 67 million years ago.

D The *Tyrannosaurus rex* is the most interesting dinosaur for many reasons.

2 Which sentence from the selection supports the author's claim that Susan Hendrickson's discovery was remarkable?

F *Located near the base of a cliff in South Dakota were the fossil remains of a dinosaur.*

G *"Sue," named after her discoverer, is considered to be the largest and best-preserved fossil of her kind.*

H *The* T. rex *was one of the last dinosaur species to live in North America, more than 67 million years ago.*

J *And with Sue's help, we continue to learn more about these amazing creatures.*

Question 1
The main idea should be connected to all the information presented in the passage. If you are having trouble coming up with the main idea, think of a short sentence that summarizes the main topic of the text.

Question 2
Not every detail in a text supports an author's argument. The text states that the *T. rex* was one of the last dinosaur species to live in North America. Does that support the argument that the discovery was remarkable, or is it an interesting detail about dinosaurs?

continued

Name_____ Date_____

Question 3

What happened to cause the scientists to realize the value of their discovery? Reread the answer choices, and then reread paragraph 1. Which one happened first in the story?

3 According to the selection, when did scientists realize the value of the fossil discovered by Susan Hendrickson?

  A after it had been studied for years

  B when it was sold for $8 million at auction

  C when it was being dug up

  D when it was moved to a museum in Chicago

Question 4

An author might choose to include an image in a selection in order to give the reader a visual and enhance the reading experience. An image does not always provide additional information, but can support the information provided in a selection.

4 The photograph is included with this selection to —

  F show how Sue looks in the Field Museum

  G prove that Sue's skeleton was really found

  H illustrate the age of Sue's skeleton

  J identify the fossil bones that were found

STAAR
STATE OF TEXAS ASSESSMENTS OF ACADEMIC READINESS

5.2(B)
Use context (e.g., in-sentence restatement) to determine or clarify the meaning of unfamiliar or multiple meaning words.

5.3(A)
Compare and contrast the themes or moral lessons of several works of fiction from various cultures.

5.6(B)
Explain the roles and functions of characters in various plots, including their relationships and conflicts.

Fig. 19(D)
Make inferences about text and use textual evidence to support understanding.

Read the selection and choose the best answer to each question.

from *The Tangled Threads*

by Eleanor H. Porter

1   To Hester, all the world seemed full of melody. Even the clouds in the sky sailed slowly along in time to a stately march in her brain, or danced to the tune of a merry polka that sounded for her ears alone.

2   Hester was forty now. Two sturdy boys and a girl of nine gave her three hungry mouths to feed and six active feet to keep in holeless stockings. Her husband had been dead two years, and life was a struggle and a problem. The boys she trained, giving just measure of love and care; but the girl—ah, Penelope should have that for which she herself had so longed. Penelope should take music lessons!

continued

3   When the piano finally arrived, Penelope was as enthusiastic as even her mother could wish her to be. It was after the child had left the house, however, that Hester came with <u>reverent step</u> into the darkened room and feasted her eyes to her heart's content on the reality of her dreams. Half fearfully she extended her hand and softly pressed the tip of her fourth finger to one of the ivory keys; then with her thumb she touched another a little below.

4   "Oh, if I only could!" she whispered, and pressed the chord again, rapturously listening to the vibrations as they died away in the quiet room. Then she tiptoed out and closed the door behind her.

Name_____ Date_____

1 Which sentence expresses a theme in the story?

A Music can be healing.

B Practice makes perfect.

C Childhood is too short.

D Joy can be found in nature.

Question 1

When determining the theme, think about an overall message the author is trying to convey through the story. Select the answer choice that best describes that message.

---

2 Which sentence from the story suggests that Hester was struggling to raise her family?

F *To Hester, all the world seemed full of melody.*

G *Her husband had been dead two years, and life was a struggle and a problem.*

H *When the piano finally arrived, Penelope was as enthusiastic as even her mother could wish her to be.*

J *"Oh, if I only could!" she whispered, and pressed the chord again, rapturously listening to the vibrations as they died away in the quiet room.*

Question 2

Reread the answers and look closely at word choice. Which sentence from the story indicates that Hester is having problems raising her family? Look for sad language (adjectives, verbs) that indicate struggle.

continued

Name_____ Date_____

Question 3

Reread the passage. Look for the details that describe the moment when Hester decides Penelope should have music lessons.

3 Why does Hester decide that Penelope should have music lessons and get a piano?

   A because Penelope asked to be able to take music lessons

   B because Hester loves music and wanted these things as a child

   C because Hester's sons are not interested in music

   D because Penelope is bored and needs a hobby

Question 4

Authors choose words carefully to show how characters are thinking and feeling. Reread the description of Hester in paragraph 3 and think about what the author is trying to tell the reader about Hester.

4 In paragraph 3, what does the phrase <u>reverent step</u> suggest about Hester's feelings?

   F She wants to be quiet at all times.

   G She thinks of the piano as a very important possession.

   H She is afraid of breaking the most expensive thing she owns.

   J She wants to keep the piano safe from her two boys.

STAAR
STATE OF TEXAS ASSESSMENTS OF ACADEMIC READINESS

Read the selection and choose the best answer to each question.

5.2(B)
Use context (e.g., in-sentence restatement) to determine or clarify the meaning of unfamiliar or multiple meaning words.

5.10(A)
Draw conclusions from the information presented by an author and evaluate how well the author's purpose was achieved.

5.11(B)
Determine the facts in text and verify them through established methods.

5.11(C)
Analyze how the organizational pattern of a text influences the relationships among the ideas.

A Discovery as Good as Gold

1   In January 1848, a sawmill worker in California named James Marshall found a glittering substance in a river. Upon closer inspection, he discovered flakes of gold floating down the current. Although he was eager to keep his discovery under wraps, it didn't stay secret for long. In March, *The Californian* reported Marshall's lucky find to the public. Although people were <u>wary</u> of the news at first, a fellow named Sam Brannan marched down the streets of San Francisco with a vial of gold dust in his hand. It was the spark that started a fire. The gold rush had commenced.

continued ➤

2   By the summer of 1848, three out of every four men from San Francisco departed from their homes in the hopes of striking it rich. Some panhandlers sifted through dirt in rivers to find flakes of gold much like Marshall and Brannan. Others risked life and limb hacking through deep mountain mines for gold ore, which was larger and much more valuable. People poured in from all over the country and headed west to mine for gold as well. Before the gold rush, there were only about 800 American citizens living in California. By the end of 1849, the population had ballooned to close to 100,000. The need for equipment, as well as food and lodging for the prospectors, helped the California economy boom in a short amount of time.

3   Of course, no enterprise is without risk. The gold rush turned out to be a gamble. Many people bet everything they owned and failed in their bid to find gold. There was something to be said for persistence, however. In 1852, the most profitable year of the gold rush, $81 million in gold was unearthed in the state.

Name_____ Date_____

1 In this selection, the author mentions the report in *The Californian* to —

   A describe how the economy of California grew quickly in a short period of time

   B point out that the most profitable year of the gold rush saw $81 million in gold unearthed

   C reveal that most people who went to California found no gold

   D explain how people found out about the discovery of gold in California

Question 1
Informational texts provide factual information that is supported by sources. What information did the report give to the people of California?

2 By organizing this selection in chronological order, the author is able to —

   F explain why few gold miners got rich

   G compare different methods of mining for gold

   H describe how the gold rush developed

   J show how foolish people were about gold

Question 2
Authors have many different ways to organize a text, include describing a sequence of events, comparing and contrasting two things, or explaining the causes and effects. In an informational text, why might it be helpful to organize information chronologically?

continued

Name_____   Date_____

Question 3

When determining the meaning of an unfamiliar word, look for context clues. In this case, the author is making a comparison that can help you understand the word. She is saying that people were cautious at first but became excited after Sam Brannan marched through the streets with his vial of gold dust.

3 In paragraph 1, the word <u>wary</u> means —

A cautious

B excited

C uninterested

D eager

Question 4

Facts can be verified through other resources, such as textbooks, encyclopedias, or academic papers. Opinions are the opposite of a fact; they often contain information about how people might have felt or thought. But opinions cannot be verified and are usually just well-informed guesses.

4 Which statement about the gold rush is a fact that can be verified?

F James Marshall was eager to keep his discovery quiet.

G Sam Brannan made a lot of people excited about gold.

H California had a population of about 100,000 by 1850.

J Many people lost hope of ever becoming rich in California.

STAAR
STATE OF TEXAS ASSESSMENTS OF ACADEMIC READINESS

5.4(A)
Analyze how poets use sound effects (e.g., alliteration, internal rhyme, onomatopoeia, rhyme scheme) to reinforce meaning in poems.

5.8(A)
Evaluate the impact of sensory details, imagery, and figurative language in literary text.

Fig. 19(D)
Make inferences about text and use textual evidence to support understanding.

Fig. 19(E)
Summarize and paraphrase texts in ways that maintain meaning and logical order within a text and across texts.

Read the selection and choose the best answer to each question.

The Dreams

by Eugene Field
from *Songs and Other Verse*

Two dreams came down to earth one night
    From the realm of mist and dew;
One was a dream of the old, old days,
    And one was a dream of the new.

5 One was a dream of a shady lane
    That led to the pickerel pond
Where the willows and rushes bowed themselves
    To the brown old hills beyond.

And the people that peopled the old-time dream
10   Were pleasant and fair to see,
And the dreamer he walked with them again
    As often of old walked he.

Oh, cool was the wind in the shady lane
    That tangled his curly hair!
15 Oh, sweet was the music the robins made
    To the springtime everywhere!

Was it the dew the dream had brought
    From yonder midnight skies,
Or was it tears from the dear, dead years
20   That lay in the dreamer's eyes?

The other dream ran fast and free,
    As the moon benignly shed
Her golden grace on the smiling face
    In the little trundle-bed.

continued ➤

25 For 't was a dream of times to come—
    Of the glorious noon of day—
 Of the summer that follows the careless spring
    When the child is done with play.

    And 't was a dream of the busy world
30   Where valorous deeds are done;
 Of battles fought in the cause of right,
    And of victories nobly won.

 It breathed no breath of the dear old home
    And the quiet joys of youth;
35 It gave no glimpse of the good old friends
    Or the old-time faith and truth.

 But 't was a dream of youthful hopes,
    And fast and free it ran,
 And it told to a little sleeping child
40   Of a boy become a man!

 These were the dreams that came one night
    To earth from yonder sky;
 These were the dreams two dreamers dreamed—
    My little boy and I.

45 And in our hearts my boy and I
    Were glad that it was so;
 He loved to dream of days to come,
    And I of long ago.

 So from our dreams my boy and I
50   Unwillingly awoke,
 But neither of his precious dream
    Unto the other spoke.

 Yet of the love we bore those dreams
    Gave each his tender sign;
55 For there was triumph in his eyes—
    And there were tears in mine!

Name_____ Date_____

1 In "The Dreams," how does the speaker's point of view affect the way he describes the first dream?

A The narrator is recalling a friend's dream; he never met the people or visited the places described.

B The narrator describes imaginary people and places he imagined while daydreaming.

C The narrator describes his own dream of people and places from his past; his recollections reveal his fondness for these memories.

D The narrator describes his own dream of his past; his memories reveal that he has led a lonely and unhappy life.

Question 1

In the first-person point of view, the narrator uses the pronouns *I*, *me*, and *we*. The reader learns about events as the narrator learns about them. In third-person point of view, *he*, *she*, and *they* are used. The narrator knows the thoughts and feelings of all characters.

2 Which of these describes the way this poem is written?

F Each stanza is a paragraph about one subject.

G The second and fourth lines of each stanza rhyme throughout the poem.

H Every pair of lines includes at least one internal rhyme.

J The poet uses onomatopoeic words to imitate natural sounds.

Question 2

Look at each answer choice and see which one fits the poem. How is each stanza structured? Internal rhyme is rhyming words within the same line of a poem. Onomatopoeia is a word whose sound is similar to the thing or action it refers to.

continued

Name_____ Date_____

Question 3

Authors choose words to evoke certain feelings and emotions. Read each of these options, paying close attention to what adjectives and verbs are used.

3 In which lines from the poem is the language intended to make the reader feel sad?

A *And the people that peopled the old-time dream*

   Were pleasant and fair to see,

B *The other dream ran fast and free,*

   As the moon benignly shed

C *Of battles fought in the cause of right,*

   And of victories nobly won.

D *For there was triumph in his eyes—*

   And there were tears in mine!

Question 4

Underline the parts of the poem that are about the son's dream. Put an asterisk (*) next to the parts that are about the father's dream. Then, summarize your findings and reread the answer choices.

4 Which of these is the best summary of the two dreaming experiences described in "The Dreams"?

F The father's dream was sorrowful. The son dreamed of future war.

G The son's dream left him feeling sad and worried. The father's dream made him look forward to the future.

H The son wanted to share the details of his dream. The father did not want to talk about what he dreamed.

J The father dreamed of the boy he once was. The son dreamed of the man he hoped to be.

STAAR
STATE OF TEXAS ASSESSMENTS OF ACADEMIC READINESS

Read the selection and choose the best answer to each question.

How to Make a Personal Budget

1   You may have seen a newspaper or Internet headline such as "Congress Passes $3.7 Trillion Budget." You may have heard that an after-school program was canceled because of "budget cuts." You may wonder just what a budget is.

2   A budget is simply a plan for how to use money. Federal, state, and local governments get money mainly through taxes. The government's budget is a plan for how to spend or save the money that is collected.

3   Individuals and families do the same thing. A budget allows people to plan for buying expensive things, such as a house, car, or refrigerator. It also helps them <u>monitor</u> what they spend on things like food, clothing, sports activities, and vacations. With a budget, people can save for expenses that are years in the future. Many parents use a budget to save for a child's college education.

4   Making a personal budget can help you understand your own money and how you spend it. It can also help you save money for things that are important to you. Here are the steps for making a personal, weekly budget.

5.2(A)
Determine the meaning of grade-level academic English words derived from Latin, Greek, or other linguistic roots and affixes.

5.11(D)
Use multiple text features and graphics to gain an overview of the contents of text and to locate information.

5.11(E)
Synthesize and make logical connections between ideas within a text and across two or three texts representing similar or different genres.

5.13(A)
Interpret details from procedural text to complete a task, solve a problem, or perform procedures.

5.13(B)
Interpret factual or quantitative information presented in maps, charts, illustrations, graphs, timelines, tables, and diagrams.

continued

Step 1: List Your Income

5   Think of all the ways that you gain money. You may get an allowance from your parents, get paid for work by your parents or others, or receive gifts on a birthday or other occasion. List all of your sources of income for an average week and add them together. Here is an example for a girl named Lia. Remember that your amounts may be very different from Lia's.

Type of Income	Amount Per Week
Allowance	$10.00
Babysitting	$15.00
Yard work and other chores	$10.00
Gifts	0
Total Income Per Week	**$35.00**

Step 2: List Your Fixed Expenses

6   Think of all the things you spend money on regularly. These are your "fixed expenses," or expenses that won't change much from one week to the next. Some expenses are necessary. These include food (like snacks after school), clothing, and housing. They are called "basic necessities." Other expenses are things you think are important but could live without. For Lia, these include paying for minutes on a cell-phone plan and a membership at the gym. Here are Lia's fixed expenses.

Type of Fixed Expense	Amount Per Week
Snacks after school	$10.00
Cell-phone minutes	$6.00
Gym membership	$2.00
Total Fixed Expenses Per Week	**$18.00**

Step 3: Subtract Your Fixed Expenses from Your Income

7   Subtract your fixed expenses from your income. The amount left over is money you can make a choice about spending or saving. It is called "discretionary income." People can use their discretion, or freedom of choice, to decide how to use the money they have. Lia found that she had $17 of discretionary income each week.

Total income per week	$35.00
Minus fixed expenses per week	−$18.00
Discretionary Income	**$17.00**

Step 4: Make Decisions about How to Use Discretionary Income

8   Lia likes to go to the movies and buy music on the Internet. She also wants to save money to go on a class trip next year. The trip will cost each student $200. She decided that she could spend about $12 each week on entertainment like movies and music and save $5 each week toward the class trip and other, unexpected expenses. She added these things to her weekly expenses.

Type of Expense	Amount Per Week
Snacks after school	$10.00
Cell-phone minutes	$6.00
Gym membership	$2.00
Entertainment—movies, music	$12.00
Class trip fund	$5.00
Total Expenses Per Week	**$35.00**

continued

Step 5: Adjust Your Budget as Necessary

9   Notice that Lia's income and expenses match exactly. In the future, if her income goes up, she can make changes in how she uses her discretionary income. If her expenses go up, she may need to find a way to make more money or reduce how much she chooses to use for her snacks, cell phone, entertainment, or savings.

10   When you make a budget, you may want to make it for a longer period of time, like a month, using the same steps. For example, you may get a gift on your birthday each year, but not in any other month. If you figure out your average expenses and income for a month, you can include special income like a gift. You can also plan for special expenses such as paying for a year's subscription for a magazine.

11   Consider keeping track of your actual income and expenses in a journal or account book. That way you can review your budget and make needed changes. It will help you avoid spending too much so you can keep saving for things you want. Your personal budget puts you in control of your money.

Name_____ Date_____

1   In paragraph 3, the word <u>monitor</u> comes from a Latin root that means —

   A   raise; increase

   B   change; modify

   C   follow guidelines or rules for

   D   watch closely; control

> **Question 1**
>
> **The Latin root *mon-* means "to remind" or "to warn." Based on this information, what does *monitor* mean?**

2   By the end of this article, what can the reader conclude about budgets?

   F   Creating a personal budget is well worth the time it takes.

   G   Parents should save for their children's education.

   H   A gym membership is more important than spending money on music.

   J   Students should earn their own money to pay for class trips.

> **Question 2**
>
> **Based on the information in this selection, what does the author want you to think about budgets? Details from the selection should support your conclusion.**

continued ➡

Name_____ Date_____

Question 3

In informational text, the headings can help you locate information because they tell you what each section of the text is about. Think about the information this question is focusing on and scan the headings in this passage. Reread the section where this information is most likely to be found.

3 According to this article, what is the first step in making a personal budget?

   A Make decisions about discretionary income.

   B List your income.

   C Subtract fixed expenses from income.

   D List your fixed expenses.

Question 4

Reread paragraph 6 and look for the word *necessary* or *necessity*. Read the surrounding sentences to find the basic necessities.

4 Which of these is a basic necessity that people should include in a budget?

   F Internet access

   G car expenses

   H housing

   J cell phone

Question 5

Use the section heads to help you figure out where to find this answer. Then reread the section, looking for details about making changes to a personal budget.

5 In which section of the article can the reader find information about making changes in a personal budget?

   A The opening paragraphs

   B Step 3

   C Step 4

   D Step 5

Read the selection and choose the best answer to each question.

STAAR
STATE OF TEXAS ASSESSMENTS OF ACADEMIC READINESS

5.3(A)
Compare and contrast the themes or moral lessons of several works of fiction from various cultures.

5.6(A)
Describe incidents that advance the story or novel, explaining how each incident gives rise to or foreshadows future events.

5.8(A)
Evaluate the impact of sensory details, imagery, and figurative language in literary text.

Fig. 19(D)
Make inferences about text and use textual evidence to support understanding.

Fig. 19(E)
Summarize and paraphrase texts in ways that maintain meaning and logical order within a text and across texts.

A Day for Fishing

1   The sun shone brightly in the turquoise sky as Nick and Enrique boarded the boat with Enrique's father, Julio. Nick was a novice at fishing and boating, but he tried to feel courageous as Julio's little vessel cruised the shining lake.

2   "In Puerto Rico," Julio told them, referring to the island where he grew up before moving to Minnesota, "we fished the ocean and caught enormous swordfish and tuna."

3   Enrique taught Nick about bait and hooks in between Julio's stories. "This lake's fish are smaller," Enrique whispered to Nick, who squirmed at Julio's description of a five-foot-long swordfish. "Most are too small, so we'll throw them back; but it's fun anyway."

4   Suddenly, the sky darkened. Over the lake, rain began to fall—first softly, then heavily.

5   Julio frowned. "We must get back to the dock quickly."

continued

6   As a crash of not-so-distant thunder shook Nick's calm, he noticed that their small boat was far from shore. Julio pointed out the dock they would head toward.

7   A nearby cluster of geese spluttered into flight. "They know the water's unsafe during a storm," Enrique said. To reassure Nick, he added, "We'll get ashore."

8   Lightning streaked overhead, and the wind whipped the water into jagged waves that smacked against their boat. Julio called directions about safety to the boys over the shouting thunder.

9   By the time they had reached the dock, secured the boat, and sprinted to a nearby shelter, they were soaked.

10   "The storm will pass; they always do," Julio smiled through hard breaths, perhaps recalling childhood memories. The three of them sat together, watching the sky flash and rage. Within several minutes, the storm cleared, leaving the lake calm again.

11   "Ready for more fishing?" Enrique asked, grinning at Nick's surprise.

12   With a deep breath, Nick gathered his courage and followed his friend back to the boat.

Name_____ Date_____

1 Why do Julio, Enrique, and Nick go back to the dock?

   A because Nick is scared

   B because a storm moves in

   C because Julio is done fishing

   D because the boys are bored

Question 1
When looking for specific details in a story, skim the text and look for key words to help you find the place in the story you need to focus on.

2 Which sentence expresses a theme of this story?

   F Hard work always pays off.

   G Sometimes we have to be brave to get what we want.

   H Friendship is more important than anything else.

   J Connecting with nature can make your problems seem small.

Question 2
When discussing theme, think about what the characters learn and the ideas that they express in the story. In "A Day for Fishing," what does Nick, the main character, learn?

3 Read this sentence from the story.

> As a crash of not-so-distant thunder shook Nick's calm, he noticed that their small boat was far from shore.

The author uses this sentence to suggest that —

   A the storm is far away

   B Nick is going to take charge

   C the storm will end soon

   D Nick is beginning to feel scared

Question 3
Think about how Nick feels before the storm and how he feels when the storm arrives. Is this sentence about the location of the storm or how the storm is affecting Nick?

continued

Name_____ Date_____

Question 4

Reread the passage and look at any descriptions that refer to Nick as well as any lines of dialogue spoken to or about him. Think about what these details reveal about his character.

4 Which sentence from the story supports the idea that Nick does not have much experience with fishing?

F *The sun shone brightly in the turquoise sky as Nick and Enrique boarded the boat with Enrique's father, Julio.*

G *"This lake's fish are smaller," Enrique whispered to Nick, who squirmed at Julio's description of a five-foot-long swordfish.*

H *As a crash of not-so-distant thunder shook Nick's calm, he noticed that their small boat was far from shore.*

J *"Ready for more fishing?" Enrique asked, grinning at Nick's surprise.*

Question 5

A summary includes only the most important parts of a story, and it is supported by details from the selection.

5 Which of these is the best summary of the story?

A Nick goes out fishing in a boat with his friend Enrique and Enrique's father. When a storm moves in, they hurry back to shore.

B Enrique tries to teach his friend Nick about fishing, but a thunderstorm begins. The boys get completely soaked in the heavy rain.

C Nick and his friend Enrique go out in a boat with Enrique's father, Julio. They catch a five-foot-long swordfish and throw it back.

D Enrique gets into a boat with his friend Nick, and they get ready to go fishing. A storm moves in before they leave the dock.

Read the selection and choose the best answer to each question.

STAAR
STATE OF TEXAS ASSESSMENTS OF ACADEMIC READINESS

5.2(A)
Determine the meaning of grade-level academic English words derived from Latin, Greek, or other linguistic roots and affixes.

5.10(A)
Draw conclusions from the information presented by an author and evaluate how well the author's purpose was achieved.

5.11(A)
Summarize the main ideas and supporting details in a text in ways that maintain meaning and logical order.

5.14(C)
Identify the point of view of media presentations.

Modern Dance

1   Modern dance was born at the start of the twentieth century in the United States. It began when a few <u>choreographers</u> and dancers rebelled against the prevailing forms of dance used at the time. Ballet was seen as rigid and imperialistic, the dance of the royal courts in Europe and Asia. Popular vaudeville shows featured entertainers who danced as part of their funny musical numbers. The desire to find a more fluid expression in dance led to a new style.

2   During the 1920s, a passion for interpretive dance swept across America. The famous dancer Isadora Duncan, known today as the mother of modern dance, introduced the idea of serious theatrical dancing to the professionals. Its purpose was to showcase emotion through dance and movement in a concert-style performance. The professionals, in turn, passed this style on to audiences. This set the stage for the next generation of modern dancers, who further developed the craft.

continued ▶

3   That's not to say that modern dance has not changed since the Great Depression. On the contrary, social and artistic upheavals in the 1960s and 1970s greatly influenced modern dance and helped it evolve. One of the biggest changes in dance was the idea of improvisation. This was a radical departure from the modern dance known forty years earlier.

4   Today's pioneers in the modern dance field have come to embrace ballet. They see ballet as the core foundation of all dancing. As a result, dance companies of all types regard fluency in all dance genres as essential. Today's modern dance is really a fusion of multiple dance genres, including those the original pioneers worked to move away from a century ago.

Name_____ Date_____

1 What is this selection mainly about?

A Isadora Duncan is known as the mother of modern dance.

B The modern dance movement has evolved since it was born in the first half of the twentieth century.

C Modern dance now incorporates ballet, which dancers rejected when the new genre first began.

D The purpose of modern dance is to showcase emotion through dance.

Question 1

Ignore answer choices that describe a single detail from the text when selecting the correct main idea.

2 Which sentence from the selection supports the idea that modern dance keeps changing?

F *Ballet was seen as rigid and imperialistic, the dance of the royal courts in Europe and Asia.*

G *The famous dancer Isadora Duncan, known today as the mother of modern dance, introduced the idea of serious theatrical dancing to the professionals.*

H *On the contrary, social and artistic upheavals in the 1960s and 1970s greatly influenced modern dance and helped it evolve.*

J *They see ballet as the core foundation of all dancing.*

Question 2

Look for words that indicate change, such as *influence, evolve, progress, alter,* and *vary.*

continued

Name_____ Date_____

Question 3

An author almost always has a purpose for writing a selection—for example, to show, explain, teach, inform, entertain, persuade, or share an experience with the reader. Think about why the author wrote this article.

Question 4

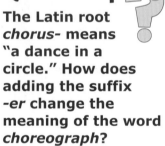

The Latin root *chorus-* means "a dance in a circle." How does adding the suffix *-er* change the meaning of the word *choreograph*?

Question 5

Visuals provide additional information about a passage. Why would the author want to include an image of dancers in an article about modern dance?

3 The author's purpose in this selection is to explain that modern dance is —

A rigid and imperialistic

B the core foundation of dancing

C a fusion of multiple genres

D the dance of European and Asian royal courts

4 In paragraph 1, the word <u>choreographers</u> comes from Latin roots that mean —

F people who compose dances

G the inventor of ballet

H entertainers in a theater

J pioneers in the dance world

5 The photo is included with this selection to —

A compare ballet and modern dance

B show what Isadora Duncan looked like

C compare the skills of male and female dancers

D show an example of modern dance

STOP!

STAAR
STATE OF TEXAS ASSESSMENTS OF ACADEMIC READINESS

5.2(B)
Use context [e.g., in-sentence restatement] to determine or clarify the meaning of unfamiliar or multiple meaning words.

Fig. 19(D)
Make inferences about text and use textual evidence to support understanding.

Read the selection and choose the best answer to each question.

Nature Girl

Characters

KAYA PHILLIPS: twelve-year-old girl

GRANDMA: Kaya's grandmother

ELI PHILLIPS: Kaya's dad, a teacher

LEAH PHILLIPS: Kaya's mother, a doctor

SCENE 1

1 [*Lights rise on a cramped apartment in New York City. KAYA sits at her desk in her room, attempting to read. The city is loud outside with the sounds of constant shouting, beeping, and screeching. She shuts her window and goes back to reading; then she sighs and walks to the living room where GRANDMA is knitting.*]

2 **KAYA:** Grandma, I can't concentrate because the noise around here is so obnoxious! [*She plops down on the couch.*] I've read the same sentence like a hundred times, and every time I try to start again, I hear a crash or someone yelling outside. I can't center my brain!

3 **GRANDMA:** [*smiles in an inviting way*] Well, this is New York—of course it's noisy outside. The hustle and bustle won't go away, but it is possible to filter what you hear.

4 **KAYA:** How do you do that, Grandma? How do you filter noise?

5 [*Before GRANDMA can answer, ELI and LEAH enter carrying take-out containers; the delicious aroma of hot food comes in with them.*]

6 **ELI:** Greetings, earthlings! Who wants Chinese food? [*KAYA laughs and jumps up.*]

7 **KAYA:** I do! This is awesome, Dad! [*ELI, LEAH, KAYA, and GRANDMA start setting the table and opening containers.*]

8 **GRANDMA:** [*to LEAH*] You know, I could have made dinner for everyone tonight. I'll bet Kaya would like some good old-fashioned pemmican and succotash, prepared the way our Iroquois ancestors used to make them.

continued

9 **LEAH:** Mom, please don't start. I had three surgeries back-to-back at the hospital today, and we had new-employee orientation. Anyway, don't knock this kind of food until you try it. The Chinese food we get is excellent—and certainly better than succotash.

10 **GRANDMA:** Oh, there's nothing like corn and bean stew, my daughter, for I am after all the Corn Mother!

11 **KAYA:** [*laughs*] Corn Mother, Grandma—who is that?

12 **ELI:** Someone pretty corny!

13 [*Simultaneously, they all laugh and sit down to eat.*]

14 **GRANDMA:** Corn Mother is part of an old tale from our Iroquois ancestors. Do you know of the woman who gave her body to the earth to save her people?

15 **KAYA:** No, I've never heard of her.

16 **GRANDMA:** Oh, my! Well, after she died, her ashes were spread over the land and eventually grew to become the source of the first corn plants. She sacrificed herself to save others, to nourish others, to keep them healthy. She symbolized healthy and nutritious food that doesn't resemble what most people eat today. [*She looks down at her plate and pushes her food around, suspiciously inspecting every angle.*]

17 **LEAH:** Mom, I promise you, the food is not poisonous. It's fresh and nourishing—and yummy!

18 **GRANDMA:** [*skeptical*] We shall see . . .

19 [*The family eats in silence while the din of the city increases and the lights dim.*]

SCENE 2

20 [*Lights rise on KAYA and GRANDMA walking around the city. They stop at a busy intersection as a bus whizzes by them, causing GRANDMA'S skirt to rustle.*]

21 **KAYA:** [*curiously*] So, Grandma, please explain again, what are we doing here?

22 **GRANDMA:** Well, to continue our conversation from yesterday, you wanted to know how to tune out the city, and I'm planning to demonstrate ways you can appreciate your surroundings without letting them overtake you. Close your eyes.

23 **KAYA:** [*incredulously*] Seriously?

24 **GRANDMA:** Yes, Kaya, just trust me.

25 [*KAYA sighs in disbelief and closes her eyes.*]

26 **GRANDMA:** What do you hear?

27 **KAYA:** A lot of noise! [*She opens her eyes.*] Come on, Grandma, this is silly! [*GRANDMA just stands there staring with quiet determination.*]

28 **KAYA:** Oh, fine! [*She closes her eyes.*] Okay, I hear buses, cars, people yelling. So? That's New York.

29 **GRANDMA:** Yes, but imagine that the whoosh of the bus is actually wind whipping up the ocean waves, and the honking is the sound of birds communicating as they fly overhead. Substitute the sounds and images of nature to restore your cheerfulness—understand?

30 **KAYA:** I think so. Could the yelling be wolf cubs wrestling or attacking?

31 **GRANDMA:** Precisely, my dear, and what else do you hear?

32 **KAYA:** The whoosh of the bus could also be a rustling cornfield or swaying leaves, and the honking could be drumbeats, and the hollering could be chanting around a campfire!

33 **GRANDMA:** Well done. Now open your eyes and look carefully; tell me, what do you see?

34 **KAYA:** A concrete jungle.

35 **GRANDMA:** [*laughs*] True, but if you look carefully, you might see that a building could be the outline of a giant mountain, or the curve of the road could be a game trail through the woods or a stream bustling through the valley.

36 **KAYA:** And the cars are canoes, and the streetlamps are lightning bugs!

continued

37 **GRANDMA:** Now you're getting it. Remember, when the city disrupts or bothers you, just listen and look for the sounds of nature. Nature can nourish you and make you feel whole. Don't forget, that's how our ancestors survived.

38 [*KAYA and GRANDMA walk home, smiling and laughing joyously, as lights fade to black.*]

Name_____ Date_____

1 Which paragraph from Scene 1 supports the idea that Kaya is having trouble living in the city?

  A *KAYA: Grandma, I can't concentrate because the noise around here is so obnoxious! [She plops down on the couch.]*

  B *GRANDMA: [smiles in an inviting way] Well, this is New York—of course it's noisy outside.*

  C *ELI: Greetings, earthlings! Who wants Chinese food? [KAYA laughs and jumps up.]*

  D *[ELI, LEAH, KAYA, and GRANDMA start setting the table and opening containers.]*

Question 1

Think about why Kaya finds New York City difficult to live in. Which answer choice describes Kaya's difficulties?

2 Which phrase from the selection gives a clue to the meaning of <u>skeptical</u> as it is used in paragraph 18?

  F *sacrificed herself to save others*

  G *suspiciously inspecting every angle*

  H *fresh and nourishing—and yummy!*

  J *while the din of the city increases and the lights dim*

Question 2

Reread paragraph 16. What part of Grandma's reaction to the food tells you the meaning of *skeptical*?

continued

Name_____ Date_____

Question 3

The theme is the main message of a story. Themes are broad ideas that can be applied to your life. They are not often stated, but must be inferred from the text.

3 Which lines express a theme of the play?

A *Anyway, don't knock this kind of food until you try it. The Chinese food we get is excellent—and certainly better than succotash.*

B *Corn Mother is part of an old tale from our Iroquois ancestors. Do you know of the woman who gave her body to the earth to save her people?*

C *Open your eyes and look carefully; tell me, what do you see?*

D *Just listen and look for the sounds of nature. Nature can nourish you and make you feel whole.*

Question 4

Make inferences about characters as you read based on what they say and do, as well as direct descriptions.

4 What inference can the reader make about Kaya and her family based on the dialogue in Scene 1?

F Kaya used to live in an Iroquois village before moving to the city.

G Grandma does not trust the food from restaurants.

H Kaya's parents and Grandma do not get along very well.

J Grandma and Kaya met for the first time last year.

Question 5

Read to the end of the play, beginning with paragraph 28. Pay close attention to the dialogue and stage directions.

5 Which paragraph from the play suggests that Kaya and Leah don't always appreciate or relate to Grandma's views about her Iroquois heritage?

A *KAYA: Grandma, I can't concentrate because the noise around here is so obnoxious!*

B *GRANDMA: [to LEAH] You know, I could have made dinner for everyone tonight.*

C *LEAH: Mom, please don't start.*

D *KAYA: And the cars are canoes, and the streetlamps are lightning bugs!*

STAAR
STATE OF TEXAS ASSESSMENTS OF ACADEMIC READINESS

5.2(B)
Use context (e.g., in-sentence restatement) to determine or clarify the meaning of unfamiliar or multiple meaning words.

5.7(A)
Identify the literary language and devices used in biographies and autobiographies, including how authors present major events in a person's life.

5.14(C)
Identify the point of view of media presentations.

Fig. 19(D)
Make inferences about text and use textual evidence to support understanding.

Read the selection and choose the best answer to each question.

Gordon Parks and His Camera

1 Gordon Parks was born in Fort Scott, Kansas, in 1912. His town was segregated, like many other parts of the United States at the time.

2 In some southern parts of the country, laws and customs forced blacks and whites to use separate schools and other public facilities. They couldn't sit in the same section in a movie theater or drink from the same water fountain. The North wasn't strictly segregated by race, but throughout the country African Americans had few economic or educational opportunities.

3 Gordon Parks felt the pain of this racism as a boy and through much of his adult life. But early on, he made an important choice. "I picked up a camera because it was my choice of weapons against what I hated most about the universe: racism, intolerance, poverty," he said. "I could have just as easily picked up a knife or a gun, like many of my childhood friends did . . . but I chose not to go that way. I felt that I could somehow subdue these evils by doing something beautiful . . . [I could] make a whole different life for myself."

4 Gordon was the youngest of fifteen children in a poor family. His parents stressed the importance of education, equality, and truth. They worked hard on their small farm and taught their children strong religious values.

5 Gordon was fifteen when his mother died. He was sent to live with a sister in St. Paul, Minnesota, but within a year, he found himself homeless. He worked at many jobs to support himself, including mopping floors, washing dishes, and playing the piano. He spent years moving from place to place, struggling to earn enough to eat and have a place to live.

continued ▶

6   Finally, in 1934, Parks found a steady job serving meals on a train from St. Paul. He married and had three children. During that time he found a magazine left behind on the train. It had photographs showing the terrible living conditions of some U.S. farmworkers.

7   Inspired by those pictures, Parks bought a camera. He took his first photos in Seattle, Washington, at the end of the train line. He was so focused on the pictures that he fell into the ocean as he tried to photograph seagulls.

Gordon Parks in 1963 at a civil rights demonstration

8   His talents soon became obvious. He worked as a fashion photographer in St. Paul. Then he moved to Chicago to do more fashion photography, but he also took his own pictures of people in the city. Those pictures won him an award and a job offer. He became the first African American photographer to work for the U.S. government <u>documenting</u> everyday American life.

9   Over the years, he received at least 45 honorary degrees from universities, even though he had never finished high school. He wrote fiction, nonfiction, and poetry books; wrote and directed movies for theaters and television; and wrote and helped produce a ballet. But it was his photography that touched millions of people around the world.

10   One series of pictures in 1961 showed a young boy in Brazil who suffered with asthma but had no money for treatment. Parks's photographs inspired thousands of dollars in donations. He was able to bring the boy to the United States for treatment that saved his life.

11   Parks photographed people and events of the African American civil rights movement from the 1950s through the 1970s. Some of his other photos persuaded American lawmakers to create programs to help people who were poor and hungry.

12   Parks called his camera his "weapon against poverty and racism." But he showed other sides of the world as well, including beautiful portraits of fashion models, artists, workers, and children. "The camera is not meant to just show misery," Parks said. "You can show beauty with it . . . . You can show things you like about the universe, things you hate about the universe. It's capable of doing both." Parks died in 2006 at the age of 93.

continued

American Gothic

1   Parks took one of his most famous photos on his first day of work in Washington, D.C. in 1942. It showed an African American woman who cleaned the floors in a government building. Parks deliberately made the photo similar to one of the most famous American paintings of the time, created in 1930 by Grant Wood. Both are titled *American Gothic.* Parks's picture showed a side of American life that few white people ever thought about.

     STAAR Reading Warm-Ups & Test Practice Grade 5 • ©2014 Newmark Learning, LLC

Name_____ Date_____

1 In this selection, the author uses paragraphs 6 and 7 to —

    A introduce Gordon Parks's family to the reader

    B explain why Gordon Parks had trouble finding a job

    C show a less serious side of Gordon Parks

    D explain how Gordon Parks got started as a photographer

> **Question 1**
> What is the main idea of paragraphs 6 and 7? What information do they provide about Gordon Parks? Focus only on those paragraphs.

2 In paragraph 8, the word <u>documenting</u> means —

    F trying to improve

    G making a record of

    H bringing about change in

    J analyzing the details of

> **Question 2**
> Think about Gordon Parks's goal as a photographer. What was he trying to do? Look for context clues in the surrounding sentences to help.

3 The author includes the two *American Gothic* photos in the selection to —

    A make readers want to see more of Parks's photos

    B identify an important person in Parks's life

    C show the kind of work Parks did

    D compare the skills of Gordon Parks and Grant Wood

> **Question 3**
> Authors feature images to provide further detail and facts. What purpose does a photographer's picture serve in a biographical text?

continued

Name_____ Date_____

Question 4

Which sentence actually describes Gordon Parks's subjects, rather than Parks himself? Find the sentences in the text to double check your answer.

4 Which sentence from the selection explains how Gordon Parks chose many of the subjects for his photographs?

F *"I felt that I could somehow subdue these evils by doing something beautiful . . ."*

G *He spent years moving from place to place, struggling to earn enough to eat and have a place to live.*

H *He worked as a fashion photographer in St. Paul.*

J *They worked hard on their small farm and taught their children strong religious values.*

Question 5

Which of these answer choices indicates that changes took place because of Gordon Parks's photographs? What effect did his photographs have on society?

5 Which sentence from the selection supports the idea that Parks's photographs helped bring about changes in society and people's lives?

A *The North wasn't strictly segregated by race, but throughout the country African Americans had few economic or educational opportunities.*

B *He was so focused on the pictures that he fell into the ocean as he tried to photograph seagulls.*

C *Then he moved to Chicago to do more fashion photography, but he also took his own pictures of people in the city.*

D *Some of his other photos persuaded American lawmakers to create programs to help people who were poor and hungry.*

Read the selection and choose the best answer to each question.

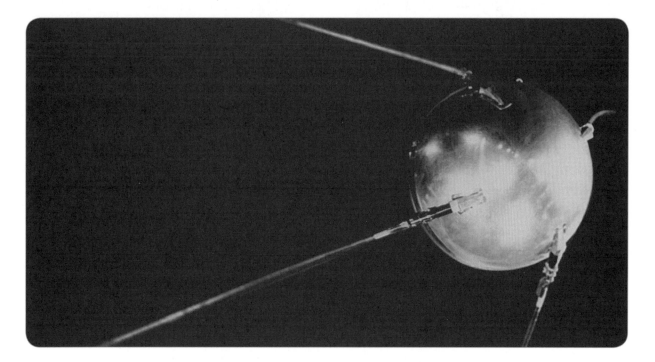

What Is a Satellite?

from www.nasa.gov/audience/forstudents/5-8/features/what-is-a-satellite-58.html

1   A satellite is a moon, planet, or machine that orbits a planet or star. For example, Earth is a satellite because it orbits the sun. Likewise, the moon is a satellite because it orbits Earth. Usually, the word *satellite* refers to a machine that is launched into space and moves around Earth or another body in space.

2   Earth and the moon are examples of natural satellites. Thousands of artificial, or man-made, satellites orbit Earth. Some take pictures of the planet that help meteorologists predict weather and track hurricanes. Some take pictures of other planets, the sun, black holes, dark matter, or faraway galaxies. These pictures help scientists better understand the solar system and universe.

continued

3   Still other satellites are used mainly for communications, such as beaming TV signals and phone calls around the world. A group of more than twenty satellites make up the Global Positioning System, or GPS. If you have a GPS receiver, these satellites can help figure out your exact location.

Why Are Satellites Important?

4   The bird's-eye view that satellites have allows them to see large areas of Earth at one time. This ability means satellites can collect more data, more quickly, than instruments on the ground.

5   Satellites also can see into space better than telescopes on Earth's surface. That's because satellites fly above the clouds, dust, and molecules in the atmosphere that can block the view from ground level.

6   Before satellites, TV signals didn't go very far. TV signals only travel in straight lines. So they would quickly trail off into space instead of following Earth's curve. Sometimes mountains or tall buildings would block them. Phone calls to faraway places were also a problem. Setting up telephone wires over long distances or underwater is difficult and costs a lot of money.

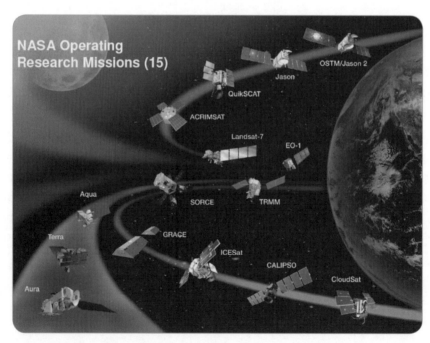

NASA has satellites orbiting Earth to study the land, oceans, and atmosphere.

7   With satellites, TV signals and phone calls are sent upward to a satellite. Then, almost instantly, the satellite can send them back down to different locations on Earth.

What Are the Parts of a Satellite?

8   Satellites come in many shapes and sizes. But most have at least two parts in common—an antenna and a power source. The antenna sends and receives information, often to and from Earth. The power source can be a solar panel or battery. Solar panels make power by turning sunlight into electricity.

9   Many NASA satellites carry cameras and scientific sensors. Sometimes these instruments point toward Earth to gather information about its land, air, and water. Other times they face toward space to collect data from the solar system and universe.

How Do Satellites Orbit Earth?

10   Most satellites are <u>launched</u> into space on rockets. A satellite orbits Earth when its speed is balanced by the pull of Earth's gravity. Without this balance, the satellite would fly in a straight line off into space or fall back to Earth. Satellites orbit Earth at different heights, different speeds, and along different paths. The two most common types of orbit are *geostationary* (jee-oh-STAY-shuh-nair-ee) and *polar*.

11   A geostationary satellite travels from west to east over the equator. It moves in the same direction and at the same rate Earth is spinning. From Earth, a geostationary satellite looks like it is standing still since it is always above the same location.

12   Polar-orbiting satellites travel in a north-south direction from pole to pole. As Earth spins underneath, these satellites can scan the entire globe, one strip at a time.

continued

Name_____ Date_____

1 What is the main idea of this selection?

   A Scientists use satellites to study space because they can fly above the clouds.

   B Some satellites use energy from the sun to stay powered while orbiting Earth.

   C Earth and the moon are examples of natural satellites that orbit larger bodies.

   D Satellites are used in many ways to help people communicate with each other and gather information.

---

2 Which sentence from the selection states a fact that can be verified?

   F *A group of more than twenty satellites make up the Global Positioning System, or GPS.*

   G *The bird's-eye view that satellites have allows them to see large areas of Earth at one time.*

   H *This ability means satellites can collect more data, more quickly, than instruments on the ground.*

   J *Satellites also can see into space better than telescopes on Earth's surface.*

Name_____ Date_____

3 Based on the information in the selection, how do satellites help
meteorologists?

    A by sending phone calls

    B by beaming TV signals

    C by taking pictures of Earth

    D by taking pictures of space

---

4 Read this dictionary entry.

> **launch** \lônch\ *verb*
> **1.** to put a boat or ship in the water **2.** to
> send forth or release **3.** to start a person on
> a course or career **4.** to start an application
> program on a computer

Which definition best matches the word <u>launch</u> as it is used in
paragraph 10?

    F Definition 1

    G Definition 2

    H Definition 3

    J Definition 4

continued

Name_____ Date_____

5 According to the selection, which of these is a use for satellites?

    A landing on and exploring other planets

    B getting rid of dust that blocks the view of Earth

    C changing the weather conditions in a given area

    D helping GPS receivers figure out locations

---

6 In which section of the article should a reader look to find information about geostationary satellites?

    F the opening paragraphs

    G Why Are Satellites Important?

    H What Are the Parts of a Satellite?

    J How Do Satellites Orbit Earth?

Name_____ Date_____

7 Which of these is a characteristic of both geostationary and polar-orbiting satellites?

    A They travel in a north-south direction.

    B They are balanced by Earth's gravity.

    C From Earth, they appear to stand still.

    D They can scan the entire globe.

8 In paragraph 4, why does the author compare the view of a satellite to that of a bird?

    F because birds can see at night

    G because birds have good eyesight

    H because birds see the world from above

    J because birds can see through large objects

continued

Name_____ Date_____

9 What inference can the reader make based on the information in the section Why Are Satellites Important?

   A Satellites will soon replace all of the telescopes used by scientists.

   B Satellites have made it cheaper to send both TV signals and phone calls.

   C Satellites are much bigger now than they were when they were invented.

   D Satellites have made it easier for people to communicate over long distances.

10 By using comparison and contrast to organize the opening paragraphs in this selection, the author is able to —

   F describe the differences between natural and artificial satellites

   G explain how satellites stay in orbit around Earth

   H describe the events that took place in the development of satellites

   J explain how the parts of a satellite send and receive data

STAAR Reading Warm-Ups & Test Practice Grade 5 • ©2014 Newmark Learning, LLC

Read the selection and choose the best answer to each question.

The Mill Girls of Lowell, Massachusetts

1   In the early 1800s, life in America began to change for many people. Most families still lived on farms, but factories were springing up. Inventors were introducing ways to use the energy of falling water to drive machinery. The Industrial Age was beginning.

2   Already, power looms in England were weaving cloth much more quickly than people could weave it at home. Americans were buying this factory-made cloth. An American named Francis Cabot Lowell visited the textile mills in England and took careful note of how the machinery worked. When he returned to America, he hired an engineer to help him create a power loom. He wanted to manufacture cloth in America. In fact, he hoped to create a new community dedicated to textile production.

continued

3   Lowell formed a company called Boston Associates. In 1814, Boston Associates built a factory in Waltham, Massachusetts. It was the first mill in the United States that combined all of the operations needed to make finished cloth from raw cotton. Once it had a successful model, Boston Associates bought some land near two rivers. There it built several textile mills powered by water. The brand-new industrial city of Lowell was born.

4   But how would the Lowell mills find enough workers? Factory work had a very bad reputation. In England, mill workers lived in desperate poverty. Hoping to build a better kind of community, the mill owners in Lowell decided to recruit young women from farms all over New England. They made the jobs attractive to these new workers. In those days, very few jobs were open to women, and women received extremely low pay. The mill owners offered higher pay. They made sure the young women would have safe, clean places to live, too. They built dormitories and boarding houses near the mills. They set up a strict schedule and rules of behavior for the workers. Bells rang to tell them when to get up, when to start work, when to take their meals, and when to go to bed.

5   Lucy Larcom was one mill worker who wrote about those early days. Lucy's father had died when she was eight. Her mother ran a boarding house in Lowell to support the family. At first, Lucy went to school while helping out at the boarding house, but the family still had too little money to survive. At age eleven, Lucy went to work as a "mill girl." Later, she wrote about her experience:

6   *I know that sometimes the <u>confinement</u> of the mill became very wearisome to me. In the sweet June weather I would lean far out of the window, and try not to hear the unceasing clash of sound inside.*

7   Mill work was dirty and noisy. The din of the mechanical looms actually caused some workers to become deaf. For Lucy, it was a daily <u>torment</u>:

8   *I loved quietness. The noise of machinery was particularly distasteful to me. But I discovered that I could so accustom myself to the noise that it became like a silence to me. And I defied the machinery to make me its slave. Its incessant discords could not drown the music of my thoughts if I would let them fly high enough. Even the long hours, the early rising, and the regularity enforced by the clangor of the bell were good discipline for one who was naturally inclined to dally and to dream, and who loved her own personal liberty with a willful rebellion against control.*

9   The mill girls sometimes worked as many as fourteen hours a day. Their hours were shorter in the winter. They used their evening hours to get an education and to improve themselves with music and art. They even wrote and published a magazine called *The Lowell Offering*.

10   In 1842, Charles Dickens, a famous writer from England, traveled to America. He went to Lowell to visit the mills. When he returned to England, he published his impressions of America, including some observations he wrote about the Lowell mills:

11   *These girls, as I have said, were all well dressed: and that phrase necessarily includes extreme cleanliness. They had serviceable bonnets, good warm cloaks, and shawls. Moreover, there were places in the mill in which they could deposit these things without injury; and there were conveniences for washing. They were healthy in appearance, many of them remarkably so, and had the manners and deportment of young women: not of degraded brutes of burden.*

12   He went on to say that many of the boarding houses had pianos and that nearly all of the young ladies belonged to circulating libraries. He said that he had read 400 pages of *The Lowell Offering*—a periodical "written exclusively by females actively employed in the mills." These facts, he said, would "startle a large class of readers" in England.

continued

Name_____ Date_____

1 Why did Francis Cabot Lowell visit the textile mills in England?

    A to copy their machinery

    B to see how mill workers lived

    C to write about the mills

    D to buy some of their textiles

---

2 Which words from paragraph 6 help the reader understand the meaning of <u>confinement</u>?

    F *know that sometimes*

    G *very wearisome to me*

    H *lean far out of the window*

    J *the unceasing clash of sound*

Name_____ Date_____

3 The author included an excerpt from Lucy Larcom's journal in this selection to —

    A entertain the reader with a humorous anecdote

    B give factual information about the Lowell mills

    C compare working in the mills with other jobs

    D give a firsthand account of what the mills were like

---

4 What inference can the reader make about Lucy Larcom from the words she wrote, as quoted in this selection?

    F Lucy enjoyed working long hours, getting up early, and sticking to a schedule.

    G When Lucy was young, the rigid mill schedule enforced by the bell caused her to feel defiant.

    H Lucy came to believe that young people should not be permitted to dally and to dream.

    J Lucy was naturally inclined to choose a life of good discipline and regular habits.

continued

Name_____ Date_____

5 The author includes a photo in this selection to —

    A show what a Lowell factory workroom looked like

    B describe the kind of cloth that was made in Lowell

    C show the work clothes that workers wore in the 1800s

    D describe the location of the Lowell mill buildings

6 In paragraph 7, the word <u>torment</u> means —

    F fact of life

    G call to action

    H symbol of hope

    J cause of suffering

Name_____ Date_____

7 Both Lucy Larcom and Charles Dickens wrote about the lives of Lowell's mill girls. How were their points of view alike?

    A They both compared America with England.

    B They both worked in the mills.

    C They both saw good qualities in Lowell mill workers' lives.

    D They both told about negative features of mill work.

8 Which detail from the selection supports the idea that many mill girls found opportunities to better themselves?

    F The workers had bells to tell them when to get up.

    G Most of the workers belonged to circulating libraries.

    H Many girls began working when they were eleven years old.

    J The girls lived in dormitories and boarding houses near the mill.

continued

Name_____ Date_____

9 According to the selection, how did the mill owners make mill jobs attractive to young women?

A They provided bonnets, warm cloaks, and shawls to all workers for free.

B They paid the women extra to join a circulating library and write for a magazine.

C They asked Charles Dickens to explain that mills in England were much worse.

D They offered higher pay than most jobs and safe, clean places to live.

10 Which of these is the best summary of the article?

F In 1814, Boston Associates built America's first textile mill in Waltham, Massachusetts. Soon afterward, the company built a whole city called Lowell with textile mills powered by water. Girls from farms in the surrounding area worked in the mills.

G Francis Cabot Lowell and his associates built America's first successful textile mill in Massachusetts in the early 1800s. They hired young women to work in the mills. The mill girls worked long hours but still found time for education and the arts.

H When Francis Cabot Lowell built a textile mill in the early 1800s, Lucy Larcom got a job there. She worked long hours and found the work difficult, but she enjoyed the money and found other ways to improve herself.

J Francis Cabot Lowell went to England in the early 1800s to see the English textile mills. The Industrial Age had already begun in England, and Lowell brought industry to America. He hired many young women to work in his factory.

Read the next two selections. Then choose the best answer to each question.

Curry Without Shortcuts

1   "Mom, we have got to make a dinner dish I just read about. It's called curry, and they say it's sweet, spicy, and savory all at once."

2   Julie had rushed into the living room holding her book open to show her mother the photo. Its caption read, "Curry: Utterly delicious, every time."

3   "Curry—that's adventurous," her mother laughed. "I've never cooked it, but I've tasted it and it's certainly a wondrous flavor."

4   Together they sorted through recipes online, selecting the one that looked easiest. Reading over the list of ingredients, Julie's mother sighed.

5   "We'll have to go to the grocery store; we don't have some of the spices to make this tonight."

6   "But, Mom," Julie objected, "why don't we just forget about those ingredients and substitute with the things we do have?"

7   Her mother agreed, and they prepared the curry as best they could with the ingredients they had. But when it was time to eat, Julie said, "This doesn't smell or taste nearly as magnificent as my book said it would be."

continued

8   A disappointed look was settling on her mother's face, too. "It isn't anything like the curry I tried at a restaurant once."

9   "I guess we shouldn't have been so impatient. It was silly to pick the easiest recipe and to leave out important ingredients," Julie said sadly.

10   At school the next day, Julie shared the story of her disappointing curry with her friend Priya.

11   "We can have curry at my house sometime," Priya offered.

12   "Your mom can make curry—real curry, with all of the right spices and recipe steps?" Julie asked, surprised.

13   "My mom can, my dad can, and my sister and I can! We can make it for you and even teach you. It's my grandma's recipe."

14   Priya invited Julie to dinner, and Julie eagerly accepted.

15   Throughout that evening, as Julie cooked with Priya, she became increasingly eager to try genuine curry. Carefully mincing ginger and measuring out coriander and cumin, Priya showed Julie each step and invited her to help. The <u>fragrant</u> aroma of spices whose names Julie hardly recognized surrounded her, and she felt her appetite growing. When dinner was finally ready and they sat down with Priya's family to eat, Julie knew she had never tasted anything similar to this before. For an anxious, fleeting moment, she feared that she might not like it after all: it was strange and new and a bit <u>intimidating</u>. But in a moment of courage, she took a rapid first bite.

16   "What do you think?" Priya asked, giggling at the smile already spreading over Julie's face.

17   Almost embarrassed at her own enthusiasm, Julie said it was just as delightful as she'd imagined.

18   "Now I know that ingredients matter, and sometimes harder recipes are worth the effort," she laughed, recalling her blunder the night before. Indulging in another large bite, she hoped she wouldn't accidentally eat so much that there would be none to share with her mother when she got home!

The Real Princess

by Hans Christian Andersen

1   There was once a Prince who wished to marry a Princess; but then she must be a real Princess. He traveled all over the world in hopes of finding such a lady; but there was always something wrong. Princesses he found in plenty; but whether they were real Princesses it was impossible for him to decide, for now one thing, now another, seemed to him not quite right about the ladies. At last he returned to his palace quite cast down, because he wished so much to have a real Princess for his wife.

2   One evening a fearful <u>tempest</u> arose, it thundered and lightened, and the rain poured down from the sky in torrents: besides, it was as dark as pitch. All at once there was heard a violent knocking at the door, and the old King, the Prince's father, went out himself to open it.

3   It was a Princess who was standing outside the door. What with the rain and the wind, she was in a sad condition; the water trickled down from her hair, and her clothes clung to her body. She said she was a real Princess.

continued

4   "Ah! We shall soon see about that!" thought the old Queen-mother; however, she said not a word of what she was going to do; but went quietly into the bedroom, took all the bed-clothes off the bed, and put three little peas on the bedstead. She then laid twenty mattresses one upon another over the three peas, and put twenty feather beds over the mattresses.

5   Upon this bed the Princess was to pass the night.

6   The next morning she was asked how she had slept. "Oh, very badly indeed!" she replied. "I have scarcely closed my eyes the whole night through. I do not know what was in my bed, but I had something hard under me, and am all over black and blue. It has hurt me so much!"

7   Now it was plain that the lady must be a real Princess, since she had been able to feel the three little peas through the twenty mattresses and twenty feather beds. None but a real Princess could have had such a delicate sense of feeling.

8   The Prince accordingly made her his wife; being now convinced that he had found a real Princess. The three peas were however put into the cabinet of curiosities, where they are still to be seen, provided they are not lost.

Name_____ Date_____

1 Which phrase from "Curry Without Shortcuts" helps the reader understand the meaning of <u>fragrant</u> in paragraph 15?

   A *measuring out coriander and cumin*

   B *aroma of spices*

   C *feared that she might not like it*

   D *strange and new*

2 In "Curry Without Shortcuts," the narrator tells the story from the point of view of —

   F Julie

   G Julie's mother

   H Priya

   J Priya's mother

3 In "Curry Without Shortcuts," how do Julie and her mother feel after making their first curry dish?

   A pleased

   B excited

   C resentful

   D discouraged

continued

Name_____ Date_____

4 How do the two cooking scenes in "Curry Without Shortcuts" fit together to provide the structure to the story?

    F They provide a comparison of two characters in the story.

    G They provide a contrast that helps show the theme of the story.

    H They show two steps leading to the solution of the conflict in the story.

    J They tell the cause of a problem and its effect on the characters in the story.

5 What happens as a result of Priya's invitation in "Curry Without Shortcuts"?

    A Julie and her mother decide to make the curry with substituted ingredients.

    B Julie asks her mother for help making a new recipe for curry.

    C Julie enjoys a curry dinner and realizes the importance of following a recipe.

    D Julie forgets to bring the leftover curry home and her mother gets upset.

6 In paragraph 15 of "Curry Without Shortcuts," the word intimidating comes from a Latin root that means —

    F very tasty

    G dull or boring

    H having strength

    J causing fear

Name_____ Date_____

7 How can the reader tell that "The Real Princess" is a fairy tale?

   A It involves a prince and princess who do not have names.

   B It tells the story of a man who wants to find a wife.

   C The events of the story took place a long time ago.

   D The main character's mother gets involved in the events.

8 Based on the story "The Real Princess," what inference can the reader make about the Prince?

   F The Prince does not like many people that he meets.

   G The Prince is clever and can find ways to tell if a woman is a real Princess.

   H The Prince believes that a real Princess has qualities that make her different from other women.

   J The Prince would be able to feel the three peas through the twenty mattresses.

9 How would "The Real Princess" be different if it were told from the point of view of the Princess?

   A The story would include more details about what the bed looked like.

   B The story would include the thoughts of all of the characters.

   C The story would include more details about the castle.

   D The story would include the thoughts of the Princess.

continued

Name_____ Date_____

10 In "The Real Princess," what is the meaning of <u>tempest</u> as it is used in paragraph 2?

    F blackout

    G flood

    H nighttime

    J storm

---

11 How is the Queen-mother different from the other characters in "The Real Princess"?

    A She does not trust other people.

    B She takes action to find the truth.

    C She thinks she is better than other people.

    D She does not want her son to get married.

Name_____ Date_____

12 In what way are the Queen-mother in "The Real Princess" and Priya in "Curry Without Shortcuts" alike?

    F They both help solve a problem.

    G They both are suspicious of strangers.

    H They both spend a lot of time with their families.

    J They both are happy when their plan is successful.

13 What lesson can be learned from both of these stories?

    A Princesses look and act differently from other women.

    B It can be frightening sometimes to try new things.

    C Curry and other foods never taste as good as they should.

    D It is worth the time and effort to do things right.

continued

Name_____ Date_____

14 In "The Real Princess," which sentence does the author use to add playful humor to the story?

    F *He traveled all over the world in hopes of finding such a lady; but there was always something wrong.*

    G *All at once there was heard a violent knocking at the door, and the old King, the Prince's father, went out himself to open it.*

    H *The Prince accordingly made her his wife; being now convinced that he had found a real Princess.*

    J *The three peas were however put into the cabinet of curiosities, where they are still to be seen, provided they are not lost.*

---

15 "The Real Princess" is mostly about a Prince who —

    A likes to invent challenging tests that people cannot pass

    B thinks he can only be happy with a certain kind of wife

    C enjoys traveling and does not wish to settle down

    D hopes to marry a woman who is just like his mother

STAAR Reading Warm-Ups & Test Practice Grade 5 • ©2014 Newmark Learning, LLC

Read the next two selections. Then choose the best answer to each question.

The Berlin Wall

1   When the people of East and West Berlin went to sleep on the night of August 12, 1961, everything was normal. They expected to wake up the next morning and travel between the two areas of the city to go to work, visit family and friends, and enjoy musical events and soccer games.

2   Instead, they woke up to find that the streets connecting the two sides of the city had been torn up. The East German army had placed concrete posts to block traffic and connected them with barbed wire. Even the telephone lines had been cut.

3   The army had begun building the Berlin Wall. Within a few years, it would stretch more than 100 miles, completely encircling the city of West Berlin. For twenty-eight years, the only way the people of East Berlin could reach West Berlin was by attempting to escape across the wall. Armed soldiers guarded it, ready to shoot any who tried to escape. East Berlin had become a prison.

continued

A Single Country Divided

4   Otto von Bismarck first <u>unified</u> twenty-five independent states under a single German constitution in 1871. Germany functioned as a single country for more than seventy years.

5   Germany was in the center of the two great World Wars in the twentieth century. After being defeated in World War I, Germany had quickly regained its military power. The victors of World War II were determined that this would not happen again. So, in 1945, they sliced Germany in half. The eastern half would be controlled by the communist Soviet Union. The western half would be governed by the United States, France, and Great Britain, known as the Allies.

6   Berlin, the capital and most important city in Germany, was located in the center of the eastern half. The Allies demanded control of the western part of the city, with the Soviet Union controlling the eastern part. West Berlin was like a tiny island surrounded by communist East Germany.

Escaping Communism

7   Within a few years, life in East Germany and West Germany became very different. With the support of the Allies, West Germany soon had a strong economy. Its people worked hard at well-paying jobs. They were able to buy products such as automobiles and refrigerators. They could travel where they wanted and vote in free elections.

8   East Germans were stuck under the communist system forced on them by the Soviet Union. Their economy was weak. The Soviet Union offered little support. People couldn't find jobs or worked for very low pay. They could not speak or travel freely and had no power to choose their own leaders.

STAAR Reading Warm-Ups & Test Practice Grade 5 • ©2014 Newmark Learning, LLC

9   Many young, talented East Germans wanted to live in West Germany or other free countries. If they could make it to West Berlin, they could fly on to a free country. By 1961, 2.5 million people had fled East Germany. In desperation, the government built a wall to prevent the people from leaving. Still, people risked their lives to escape. About 5,000 people succeeded, although hundreds of others were captured or killed. East Germany, supported by the Soviet Union, continually strengthened the wall to prevent escapes. Eventually, the concrete was about twelve feet high and four feet thick. A smooth pipe at the top prevented people from climbing over it.

A Dramatic Ending

10   By 1989, communism was failing across Europe. When some neighboring countries overthrew communism, East Germans gained new ways to escape. The East German government faced increasing opposition.

11   On the evening of November 9, 1989, a German official mistakenly announced that people could pass through the wall whenever they wanted. Thousands of people went to the checkpoints that night and demanded to be let through. The guards were unprepared and eventually opened the gates. Within hours, a huge celebration began on both sides of the wall. People sang and cried in joy. They chipped pieces from the concrete wall with hammers and saved the pieces as reminders of the hard times they had endured.

12   Germany soon became a united country once again. The Berlin Wall has been removed. Signs and exhibits mark the location, reminding visitors of the time when Berlin and the rest of Germany were divided. This place reminds us that many people risked their lives for freedom.

continued

Tear Down This Wall!

1   In 1981, Ronald Reagan became the fortieth president of the United States. Many believe that one of Reagan's <u>major</u> accomplishments was helping reunite a divided Germany. This was a result of historic peace talks between Reagan and Mikhail Gorbachev, the leader of the Soviet Union.

2   Reagan had a long history of speaking out against the Soviet Union and communism. He did so during his two terms as governor of California, as well as during his presidency. However, in his second term as president, Reagan began to believe that improved communication was possible. For many years, there were strained relations between the United States and the Soviet Union. Reagan was instrumental in bringing the two countries together. Reagan and Gorbachev signed a peace treaty during a period of new openness and freedom in Russia known as *glasnost*. The Intermediate-Range Nuclear-Force Missile Treaty (INF Treaty) played a large role in ending the Cold War. With this treaty, intermediate nuclear forces were reduced.

3   During the talks, Gorbachev visited the United States and Reagan traveled to the Soviet Union four times between 1985 and 1988. On one memorable trip in 1987, Reagan visited the famous Berlin Wall in Germany. The wall had been built to separate East and West Berlin. It blocked people from East Germany who were trying to migrate west. In his speech at the wall, Reagan made an emotional plea to Gorbachev:

4   *. . . in the West today, we see a free world that has achieved a level of prosperity and well-being unprecedented in all human history. In the Communist world, we see failure, technological backwardness, declining standards of health, even want of the most basic kind—too little food. Even today, the Soviet Union still cannot feed itself. After these four decades, then, there stands before the entire world one great and inescapable conclusion: Freedom leads to prosperity.*

   STAAR Reading Warm-Ups & Test Practice Grade 5 • ©2014 Newmark Learning, LLC

5   *Freedom replaces the ancient hatreds among the nations with comity and peace. Freedom is the victor. And now the Soviets themselves may, in a limited way, be coming to understand the importance of freedom. We hear much from Moscow about a new policy of reform and openness. Some political prisoners have been released. Certain foreign news broadcasts are no longer being jammed. Some economic enterprises have been permitted to operate with greater freedom from state control. Are these the beginnings of profound changes in the Soviet state? Or are they token gestures, intended to raise false hopes in the West, or to strengthen the Soviet system without changing it?*

6   *We welcome change and openness; for we believe that freedom and security go together, that the advance of human liberty can only strengthen the cause of world peace. There is one sign the Soviets can make that would be unmistakable, that would advance dramatically the cause of freedom and peace.*

7 *General Secretary Gorbachev, if you seek peace, if you seek prosperity for the Soviet Union and Eastern Europe, if you seek liberalization: Come here to this gate! Mr. Gorbachev, open this gate! Mr. Gorbachev, tear down this wall!*

8   This section of Reagan's speech was controversial because people were afraid that it could encourage war. Violence did not occur, but his plea did strike a chord with people in the Soviet Union. There was already a movement growing toward freedom, and Reagan's speech propelled it forward. Many see it as a turning point in the Cold War.

9   Although it took another two-and-a-half years, finally, in 1989, after the end of Reagan's presidency, East Germany opened the Berlin Wall to citizens and travelers. In September 1990, Reagan visited the site of the Berlin Wall to swing a hammer at a broken piece of wall as a symbol of tearing down barriers and opening the gates to freedom.

continued

Name_____ Date_____

1 In paragraph 4 of "The Berlin Wall," the word <u>unified</u> comes from a Latin root that means —

   A conquered

   B ruled

   C made into one

   D freed from prison

2 Which sentence from "The Berlin Wall" supports the idea that the Soviet Union wanted to stop people from leaving East Germany?

   F *Instead, they woke up to find that the streets connecting the two sides of the city had been torn up.*

   G *For twenty-eight years, the only way the people of East Germany could reach West Berlin was by attempting to escape across the wall.*

   H *Germany functioned as a single country for more than seventy years.*

   J *Germany was in the center of the two great World Wars in the twentieth century.*

3 How does the author of "The Berlin Wall" support the point that there were many reasons why people in East Germany wanted to move to West Germany?

   A by describing details of daily life in East and West Germany

   B by contrasting the jobs and freedoms in East and West Germany

   C by comparing life before and after East and West Germany were separated

   D by stating where people could go once they left East Germany for West Germany

Name_____ Date_____

4 According to "The Berlin Wall," why did the victors of World War II divide Germany in half?

F They wanted Germany to be separated like Berlin.

G They wanted part of Germany to be just like the Soviet Union.

H They wanted to stop Germany from becoming powerful again.

J They wanted to return Germany to the way it was before World War I.

5 Which sentence from "The Berlin Wall" states a fact that can be verified?

A *East Berlin had become a prison.*

B *Its people worked hard at well-paying jobs.*

C *They could travel where they wanted and vote in free elections.*

D *By 1961, 2.5 million people had fled East Germany.*

6 Read this dictionary entry.

> **major** \mā' jər\
> *noun* **1.** a military officer above a captain **2.** a field of study or subject that a student specializes in *adjective* **3.** of great importance **4.** of great risk; serious

Which definition best matches the word <u>major</u> as it is used in paragraph 1 of "Tear Down This Wall!"?

F Definition 1

G Definition 2

H Definition 3

J Definition 4

continued

Name_____ **Date**_____

7 According to "Tear Down This Wall!" why were the peace talks between Reagan and Gorbachev "historic"?

    A They happened many years ago.

    B They helped bring about great change in the world.

    C They took place between the United States and the Soviet Union.

    D They continued the work Reagan had begun as governor of California.

---

8 Which sentence should be included in a summary of "Tear Down This Wall!"?

    F The Berlin Wall was built at the end of World War II.

    G Reagan and Gorbachev met several times between 1985 and 1988.

    H During a trip to Berlin, Reagan asked Gorbachev to tear down the Berlin Wall.

    J Reagan's achievements made him a great president.

---

9 According to "The Berlin Wall," why did East Germans want to escape to West Germany?

    A They wanted to follow their religious beliefs.

    B They wanted to fly to the United States.

    C They wanted to show support for President Reagan.

    D They wanted freedom and economic opportunity.

STAAR Reading Warm-Ups & Test Practice Grade 5 • ©2014 Newmark Learning, LLC

Name_____ Date_____

10 What was President Reagan's main point in his "Tear Down This Wall!" speech?

F Freedom leads to economic success.

G Nothing is as important as world peace.

H Foreign news broadcasts are important.

J People in the West have false hopes.

11 Which detail from Reagan's speech in "Tear Down This Wall!" uses exaggeration to make a point?

A *. . . in the West today, we see a free world . . .*

B *In the Communist world, we see failure, technological backwardness . . .*

C *. . . coming to understand the importance of freedom.*

D *There is one sign the Soviets can make that would be unmistakable . . .*

12 What inference can be made about the author's opinion of Ronald Reagan in "Tear Down This Wall!"?

F The author likes Reagan but did not like the speech he made.

G The author admires Reagan and thinks he did an important thing.

H The author dislikes Reagan and believes his speech was a huge mistake.

J The author does not think Reagan understood the Soviet government.

continued

Name_____ **Date**_____

13 In both "The Berlin Wall" and "Tear Down This Wall!" the authors organize and present information mainly by —

   A explaining events in order of their importance

   B telling what happened in chronological order

   C asking questions and giving the answers

   D describing a problem and its solution

---

14 What is the main focus in both of these selections?

   F the Soviet Union

   G President Reagan

   H the Berlin Wall

   J East Germany

---

15 The author includes a photo in "The Berlin Wall" to —

   A show what the wall looked like

   B prove that a wall was built

   C compare East and West Berlin

   D show the soldiers of East Germany

STAAR Reading Warm-Ups & Test Practice Grade 5 • ©2014 Newmark Learning, LLC

Read the next two selections. Then choose the best answer to each question.

from *The Call of the Wild*

by Jack London

1   A dog named Buck lived the first four years of his life happily on an estate in California owned by Judge Miller. But then gold was discovered in the Klondike area of Canada, and there was a large demand for strong dogs to pull sleds through the ice and snow to the gold fields. Manuel, a man who worked for Judge Miller, decided he could make some money by kidnapping and selling Buck.

2   The Judge was at a meeting of the Raisin Growers' Association, and the boys were busy organizing an athletic club, on the memorable night of Manuel's <u>treachery</u>. No one saw him and Buck go off through the orchard on what Buck imagined was merely a stroll. And with the exception of a solitary man, no one saw them arrive at the little flag station known as College Park. This man talked with Manuel, and money chinked between them.

3   "You might wrap up the goods before you deliver 'm," the stranger said gruffly, and Manuel doubled a piece of stout rope around Buck's neck under the collar.

4   "Twist it, an' you'll choke 'm plentee," said Manuel, and the stranger grunted a ready affirmative.

5   Buck had accepted the rope with quiet dignity. To be sure, it was an unwonted performance: but he had learned to trust in men he knew, and to give them credit for a wisdom that outreached his own. But when the ends of the rope were placed in the stranger's hands, he growled menacingly. He had merely intimated his displeasure, in his pride believing that to intimate was to command. But to his surprise the rope tightened around his neck, shutting off his breath. In quick rage he sprang at the man, who met him halfway, grappled him close by the throat, and with a deft twist threw him over on his back. Then the rope tightened mercilessly, while Buck struggled in a fury, his tongue lolling out of his mouth and his great chest panting futilely. Never in all his life had he been so vilely treated, and never in all his life had he been so angry. But his strength ebbed, his eyes glazed, and he knew nothing when the train was flagged and the two men threw him into the baggage car.

continued ➤

6   The next he knew, he was dimly aware that his tongue was hurting and that he was being jolted along in some kind of a conveyance. The hoarse shriek of a locomotive whistling at a crossing told him where he was. He had travelled too often with the Judge not to know the sensation of riding in a baggage car. He opened his eyes, and into them came the unbridled anger of a kidnapped king. The man sprang for his throat, but Buck was too quick for him. His jaws closed on the hand, nor did they relax till his senses were choked out of him once more.

7   "Yep, has fits," the man said, hiding his mangled hand from the baggageman, who had been attracted by the sounds of struggle. "I'm takin' 'm up for the boss to 'Frisco. A crack dog-doctor there thinks that he can cure 'm."

8   Concerning that night's ride, the man spoke most eloquently for himself, in a little shed back of a saloon on the San Francisco water front.

9   "All I get is fifty for it," he grumbled; "an' I wouldn't do it over for a thousand, cold cash."

10   His hand was wrapped in a bloody handkerchief, and the right trouser leg was ripped from knee to ankle.

11   "How much did the other mug get?" the saloon-keeper demanded.

12   "A hundred," was the reply. "Wouldn't take a sou less, so help me."

13   "That makes a hundred and fifty," the saloon-keeper
calculated; "and he's worth it, or I'm a squarehead."

14   The kidnapper undid the bloody wrappings and looked at his
lacerated hand. "If I don't get the hydrophoby—"

15   "It'll be because you was born to hang," laughed the saloon-
keeper. "Here, lend me a hand before you pull your freight,"
he added.

16   Dazed, suffering intolerable pain from throat and tongue,
with the life half throttled out of him, Buck attempted to face his
tormentors. But he was thrown down and choked repeatedly, till
they succeeded in filing the heavy brass collar from off his neck.
Then the rope was removed, and he was flung into a cagelike
crate.

17   There he lay for the remainder of the weary night, nursing
his wrath and wounded pride. He could not understand what it all
meant. What did they want with him, these strange men? Why
were they keeping him pent up in this narrow crate? He did not
know why, but he felt oppressed by the vague sense of impending
calamity. Several times during the night he sprang to his feet when
the shed door rattled open, expecting to see the Judge, or the
boys at least. But each time it was the bulging face of the saloon-
keeper that peered in at him by the sickly light of a tallow candle.
And each time the joyful bark that trembled in Buck's throat was
twisted into a savage growl.

continued

Thor's Hammer

1   A long time ago in the northern countries of Scandinavia, when the clouds rumbled and lightning crackled across the sky, people blamed Thor, the Norse god of thunder, and his hammer, Mjöllnir. This hammer was so powerful that it could crush a mountain in a single blow. Thor was likely to fling his hammer at the least provocation. The hammer never missed its target and, incredibly, it flew back to Thor's fist when its work was done.

2   People throughout the land feared eruptions of Thor's temper—until his hammer was stolen. Without it, Thor was almost helpless; he could neither smash mountains nor subdue his enemies. Thor angrily blamed the trickster god named Loki, who was fond of pranks.

3   "I didn't take your hammer, but I know where it is," Loki confessed. "It is in the land of the Frost Giants."

4   Thrym, the Frost Giant king, had managed to steal Thor's hammer. He sent a message that he would return the hammer on one condition: Freya the Fair, goddess of love and beauty, must agree to marry him. Freya was daughter of Odin, the king of the gods. She threw herself at her father's feet and begged, "Please don't send me to the land of the Frost Giants!"

5   "Without Thor's hammer we will never be safe," Loki declared.

6   The gods of Asgard agreed and pondered just what Thor should do to get his hammer back.

7   Finally Odin, king of the gods, spoke. "Thor will travel in disguise to the land of the Frost Giants and, once there, he will steal back the hammer."

8   "In disguise?" asked Thor.

9   "Yes, disguised as Freya, bride of Thrym," commanded Odin.

10   At first Thor refused outright. But after much discussion, he realized there was no other way to retrieve his hammer. Finally, Loki offered to go along with Thor to the land of the Frost Giants disguised as Freya's maid.

11   Loki dressed Thor in Freya's velvet robes and draped Thor's enormous wrists with gems. He veiled Thor's angry, bearded face. The gods hid their laughter as Thor and Loki departed for the land of the Frost Giants.

12   Deep within the earth, the Frost Giants leaned on banquet tables heavily laden with fish and fowl, fruit, and sweetmeats. When Thor and Loki entered the banquet hall, Thrym rose to greet his bride. He reached for Thor's hand, which trembled in rage.

13   "Do not be afraid," urged Thrym.

14   Loki explained, "It is nervous anticipation that makes Freya quiver. She has long looked forward to this day."

15   Thrym swept the gnawed bones from the table with a hairy arm and patted the cushion beside him. He called a servant to bring more food.

16   Thor sat down without saying a word. He helped himself to half an ox and seven wedding cakes and began to eat.

continued

17   Thrym's eyes grew wide. He peered lovingly at his bride-to-be. "Pray tell, why are you so hungry? A tiny damsel does not usually eat so heartily."

18   Loki answered quickly, "Freya was so excited that she could not eat for eight days, but now she is <u>ravenous</u>."

19   Next, Thrym lifted the veil that covered Thor's face. Again he wondered, "Pray tell, why are your eyes like burning rubies?" Of course, Thor was furious by this point, and his eyes glowed like fiery red coals.

20   Again, Loki responded, "Why, she was so excited to meet you that she has not slept for eight days!"

21   Thrym stamped his scepter on the floor. He could wait no longer to wed Freya the Fair. "Bring Thor's hammer," he commanded.

22   No sooner had Thrym's servant fetched the hammer than Thor snatched it away. Armed with the hammer, he kept the Frost Giants at bay as he and Loki backed away and escaped from the banquet hall.

23   "Let us never speak of this humiliation again," said Thor to Loki as he ripped the veil from his face. He struck the hammer three times against a rock. His chariot appeared and carried them safely back to Asgard.

24   The hammer never again left his side. And Loki knew better than to tease Thor ever again.

Name_____ Date_____

1 In the selection from *The Call of the Wild*, what is the meaning of the word <u>treachery</u> as it is used in paragraph 2?

   A loss of faith

   B escape from a place

   C agreement

   D act of betrayal

2 Based on this selection, what event in history provided a reason for this story?

   F Gold was discovered in the Klondike.

   G Settlers moved west to California.

   H The War Between the States began.

   J The United States signed a treaty with Canada.

3 Why did Manuel kidnap Buck?

   A Buck was mean and could not be tamed.

   B He planned to sell Buck as a sled dog.

   C The Judge wanted to get rid of Buck.

   D He was afraid Buck would bite him.

continued

Name_____ Date_____

4 In the selection from *The Call of the Wild*, which sentence shows that the man who takes Buck to San Francisco regrets what he has done?

F *"Yep, has fits," the man said, hiding his mangled hand from the baggageman, who had been attracted by the sounds of struggle.*

G *Concerning that night's ride, the man spoke most eloquently for himself, in a little shed back of a saloon on the San Francisco water front.*

H *"All I get is fifty for it," he grumbled; "an' I wouldn't do it over for a thousand, cold cash."*

J *His hand was wrapped in a bloody handkerchief, and the right trouser leg was ripped from knee to ankle.*

5 How does the narrative point of view in this selection from *The Call of the Wild* affect the reader's experience with the story?

A The reader knows how the men look and act but not what happens to the dog.

B The reader learns how Buck feels and thinks, and how he reacts to each event.

C The reader experiences the story from Manuel's point of view.

D The reader relates to the men more closely than to the dog.

6 What can the reader infer from the illustration in the selection from *The Call of the Wild*?

F The train car Buck rode in was cold and dark.

G Buck was not strong enough to pull a dog sled.

H The man who took Buck could not control him.

J Buck was mistreated by the men who took him.

Name_____ Date_____

7 Which sentence from *The Call of the Wild* helps the reader understand how Buck feels about the way he is treated?

    A *Then the rope tightened mercilessly, while Buck struggled in a fury, his tongue lolling out of his mouth and his great chest panting futilely.*

    B *But his strength ebbed, his eyes glazed, and he knew nothing when the train was flagged and the two men threw him into the baggage car.*

    C *He had travelled too often with the Judge not to know the sensation of riding in a baggage car.*

    D *Then the rope was removed, and he was flung into a cagelike crate.*

8 Which of these is the best summary of the selection from *The Call of the Wild?*

    F Judge Miller went to a meeting one night. A man named Manuel worked for Judge Miller. Manuel took Judge Miller's dog for a walk.

    G Manuel worked in California on an estate. He had a dog named Buck. When Manuel decided to go to Canada to mine for gold, he took Buck with him on the train.

    H A dog named Buck was taken from Judge Miller's estate. Buck was sold, put into a cage, and loaded onto a train. A man tried to control the dog, but Buck fought hard.

    J Manuel and Buck took a walk to the train station. A man with a rope and a club attacked them and kidnapped the dog. The man put Buck in a cage on a train.

continued

Name_____ Date_____

9 In "Thor's Hammer," which phrase helps the reader understand the meaning of <u>ravenous</u> in paragraph 18?

   A *nervous anticipation that makes Freya quiver*

   B *swept the gnawed bones from the table*

   C *called a servant to bring more food*

   D *could not eat for eight days*

10 According to the selection, Thor and his hammer created what natural phenomenon?

   F mountains

   G frost

   H thunder

   J oxen

11 In "Thor's Hammer," why do the gods hide their laughter as Thor and Loki depart for the land of the Frost Giants?

   A They played a trick on Thor.

   B They do not want to hurt Thor's feelings.

   C They think Thor will refuse to go.

   D They are afraid of Thor's wrath.

Name_____ Date_____

12 In "Thor's Hammer," why doesn't Thrym realize that his "bride" is actually Thor disguised as Freya?

   F He does not get close enough to have a good look at Thor.

   G He believes the excuses Loki offers to his questions.

   H He does not want to seem foolish in front of the other Frost Giants.

   J The lighting in the banquet hall is too dim to see Thor.

13 In paragraph 19 of "Thor's Hammer," the author compares Thor's eyes to "fiery red coals" to —

   A make Thor seem attractive

   B emphasize Loki's cleverness

   C explain why Thrym was fooled

   D show how angry Thor was

continued

Name_____ Date_____

14 In "Thor's Hammer," how does the narrator's point of view influence the story?

  F The narrator makes the reader feel afraid of Thor.

  G The narrator seems to suggest that people who believe in myths are foolish.

  H The narrator makes Thor seem heroic by favoring him over the other gods.

  J The narrator presents the tale as if the gods and goddesses are real.

---

15 In "Thor's Hammer," the author includes an illustration to —

  A show how strong Thor is

  B compare Thor and the trickster Loki

  C show what Thor looks like in disguise

  D suggest that Thor really does look like Freya

Answer Key

Warm-Up 1 • Grandpa's Garden

Question & Answer	Standard
1 Read this dictionary entry. **duck** \duk\ *noun* **1.** a web-footed swimming bird *verb* **2.** to stoop or bend suddenly **3.** to avoid or evade something; to dodge **4.** to dip or plunge into the water Which definition best matches the word <u>duck</u> as it is used in paragraph 3? A Definition 1 **B Definition 2** C Definition 3 D Definition 4	**5.2(E)**
2 How does Jayden become interested in gardening? F by watching basketball players on TV G by reading a book about growing watermelons H by finding an old garden plot in the backyard **J by looking at photos of his grandfather**	**5.6(A)**
3 Which sentence from the story best shows that Grandma is pleased about Jayden starting to garden? A *"Your granddaddy definitely had a green thumb."* B *"Every day he watered, hoed, pulled weeds, and tended the garden."* C *"How about you do it?" she said brightly.* **D *"I'll turn on the hose and get the hoe!" Grandma said, exuberant.***	**5.6(B)**
4 Who is the narrator of this story? **F an outside observer** G Jayden H Grandma J Grandpa	**5.6(C)**

Warm-Up 2 • Meet Sue

Question & Answer	Standard
1 What is the main idea of this selection? **A** **The discovery of a *Tyrannosaurus rex* skeleton in 1990 was a valuable find for scientists.** B The *Tyrannosaurus rex* skeleton found in 1990 was bought for $8 million by a museum in Chicago. C The *Tyrannosaurus rex* lived in North America more than 67 million years ago. D The *Tyrannosaurus rex* is the most interesting dinosaur for many reasons.	**5.11(A)**
2 Which sentence from the selection supports the author's claim that Susan Hendrickson's discovery was remarkable? F *Located near the base of a cliff in South Dakota were the fossil remains of a dinosaur.* **G** ***"Sue," named after her discoverer, is considered to be the largest and best-preserved fossil of her kind.*** H *The T. rex was one of the last dinosaur species to live in North America, more than 67 million years ago.* J *And with Sue's help, we continue to learn more about these amazing creatures.*	**5.10(A)**
3 According to the selection, when did scientists realize the value of the fossil discovered by Susan Hendrickson? A after it had been studied for years B when it was sold for $8 million at auction **C** **when it was being dug up** D when it was moved to a museum in Chicago	**5.11(C)**
4 The photograph is included with this selection to — **F** **show how Sue looks in the Field Museum** G prove that Sue's skeleton was really found H illustrate the age of Sue's skeleton J identify the fossil bones that were found	**5.14(C)**

Warm-Up 3 • from *The Tangled Threads*

Question & Answer	Standard
1 Which sentence expresses a theme in the story? **A** **Music can be healing.** B Practice makes perfect. C Childhood is too short. D Joy can be found in nature.	**5.3(A)**
2 Which sentence from the story suggests that Hester was struggling to raise her family? F *To Hester, all the world seemed full of melody.* **G** ***Her husband had been dead two years, and life was a struggle and a problem.*** H *When the piano finally arrived, Penelope was as enthusiastic as even her mother could wish her to be.* J *"Oh, if I only could!" she whispered, and pressed the chord again, rapturously listening to the vibrations as they died away in the quiet room.*	**5.6 Fig. 19(D)**
3 Why does Hester decide that Penelope should have music lessons and get a piano? A because Penelope asked to be able to take music lessons **B** **because Hester loves music and wanted these things as a child** C because Hester's sons are not interested in music D because Penelope is bored and needs a hobby	**5.6(B)**
4 In paragraph 3, what does the phrase <u>reverent step</u> suggest about Hester's feelings? F She wants to be quiet at all times. **G** **She thinks of the piano as a very important possession.** H She is afraid of breaking the most expensive thing she owns. J She wants to keep the piano safe from her two boys.	**5.2(B)**

Warm-Up 4 • A Discovery as Good as Gold

Question & Answer	Standards
1 In this selection, the author mentions the report in *The Californian* to – A describe how the economy of California grew quickly in a short period of time B point out that the most profitable year of the gold rush saw $81 million in gold unearthed C reveal that most people who went to California found no gold **D explain how people found out about the discovery of gold in California**	**5.10(A)**
2 By organizing this selection in chronological order, the author is able to – F explain why few gold miners got rich G compare different methods of mining for gold **H describe how the gold rush developed** J show how foolish people were about gold	**5.11(C)**
3 In paragraph 1, the word <u>wary</u> means – **A cautious** B excited C uninterested D eager	**5.2(B)**
4 Which statement about the gold rush is a fact that can be verified? F James Marshall was eager to keep his discovery quiet. G Sam Brannan made a lot of people excited about gold. **H California had a population of about 100,000 by 1850.** J Many people lost hope of ever becoming rich in California.	**5.11(B)**

Warm-Up 5 • The Dreams

Question & Answer	Standard
1 In "The Dreams," how does the speaker's point of view affect the way he describes the first dream? A The narrator is recalling a friend's dream; he never met the people or visited the places described. B The narrator describes imaginary people and places he imagined while daydreaming. **C The narrator describes his own dream of people and places from his past; his recollections reveal his fondness for these memories.** D The narrator describes his own dream of his past; his memories reveal that he has led a lonely and unhappy life.	**5.4 Fig. 19(D)**
2 Which of these describes the way this poem is written? F Each stanza is a paragraph about one subject. **G The second and fourth lines rhyme throughout the poem.** H Every pair of lines includes at least one internal rhyme. J The poet uses onomatopoeic words to imitate natural sounds.	**5.4(A)**
3 In which lines from the poem is the language intended to make the reader feel sad? A *And the people that peopled the old-time dream* *Were pleasant and fair to see,* B *The other dream ran fast and free,* *As the moon benignly shed* C *Of battles fought in the cause of right,* *And of victories nobly won.* **D *For there was triumph in his eyes—*** ***And there were tears in mine!***	**5.8(A)**
4 Which of these is the best summary of the two dreaming experiences described in "The Dreams"? F The father's dream was sorrowful. The son dreamed of future war. G The son's dream left him feeling sad and worried. The father's dream made him look forward to the future. H The son wanted to share the details of his dream. The father did not want to talk about what he dreamed. **J The father dreamed of the boy he once was. The son dreamed of the man he hoped to be.**	**5.4 Fig. 19(E)**

Warm-Up 6 • How to Make a Personal Budget

Question & Answer	Standard
1 In paragraph 3, the word <u>monitor</u> comes from a Latin root that means – A raise; increase B change; modify C follow guidelines or rules for **D watch closely; control**	**5.2(A)**
2 By the end of this article, what can the reader conclude about budgets? **F Creating a personal budget is well worth the time it takes.** G Parents should save for their children's education. H A gym membership is more important than spending money on music. J Students should earn their own money to pay for class trips.	**5.11(E)**
3 According to this article, what is the first step in making a personal budget? A Make decisions about discretionary income. **B List your income.** C Subtract fixed expenses from income. D List your fixed expenses.	**5.13(A)**
4 Which of these is a basic necessity that people should include in a budget? F Internet access G car expenses **H housing** J cell phone	**5.13(B)**
5 In which section of the article can the reader find information about making changes in a personal budget? A the opening paragraphs B Step 3 C Step 4 **D Step 5**	**5.11(D)**

Warm-Up 7 • A Day for Fishing

Question & Answer	Standard
1 Why do Julio, Enrique, and Nick go back to the dock? A because Nick is scared **B because a storm moves in** C because Julio is done fishing D because the boys are bored	5.6(A)
2 Which sentence expresses a theme of this story? F Hard work always pays off. **G Sometimes we have to be brave to get what we want.** H Friendship is more important than anything else. J Connecting with nature can make your problems seem small.	5.3(A)
3 Read this sentence from the story *As a crash of not-so-distant thunder shook Nick's calm, he noticed that their small boat was far from shore.* The author uses this sentence to suggest that — A the storm is far away B Nick is going to take charge C the storm will end soon **D Nick is beginning to feel scared**	5.8(A)
4 Which sentence from the story supports the idea that Nick does not have much experience with fishing? F *The sun shone brightly in the turquoise sky as Nick and Enrique boarded the boat with Enrique's father, Julio.* **G *"This lake's fish are smaller," Enrique whispered to Nick, who squirmed at Julio's description of a five-foot-long swordfish.***** H *As a crash of not-so-distant thunder shook Nick's calm, he noticed that their small boat was far from shore.* J *"Ready for more fishing?" Enrique asked, grinning at Nick's surprise.*	5.6 Fig. 19(D)
5 Which of these is the best summary of the story? **A Nick goes out fishing in a boat with his friend Enrique and Enrique's father. When a storm moves in, they hurry back to shore.** B Enrique tries to teach his friend Nick about fishing, but a thunderstorm begins. The boys get completely soaked in the heavy rain. C Nick and his friend Enrique go out in a boat with Enrique's father, Julio. They catch a five-foot-long swordfish and throw it back. D Enrique gets into a boat with his friend Nick, and they get ready to go fishing. A storm moves in before they leave the dock.	5.6 Fig. 19(E)

Warm-Up 8 • Modern Dance

Question & Answer	Standards
1 What is this selection mainly about?	**5.11(A)**
A Isadora Duncan is known as the mother of modern dance. **B The modern dance movement has evolved since it was born in the first half of the twentieth century.** C Modern dance now incorporates ballet, which dancers rejected when the new genre first began. D The purpose of modern dance is to showcase emotion through dance.	
2 Which sentence from the selection supports the idea that modern dance keeps changing?	**5.11(A)**
F *Ballet was seen as rigid and imperialistic, the dance of the royal courts in Europe and Asia.* G *The famous dancer Isadora Duncan, known today as the mother of modern dance, introduced the idea of serious theatrical dancing to the professionals.* **H *On the contrary, social and artistic upheavals in the 1960s and 1970s greatly influenced modern dance and helped it evolve.*** J *They see ballet as the core foundation of all dancing.*	
3 The author's purpose in this selection is to explain that modern dance is —	**5.10(A)**
A rigid and imperialistic B the core foundation of dancing **C a fusion of multiple genres** D the dance of European and Asian royal courts	
4 In paragraph 1, the word <u>choreographers</u> comes from Greek roots that mean —	**5.2(A)**
F people who compose dances G the inventor of ballet H entertainers in a theater J pioneers in the dance world	
5 The photo is included with this selection to —	**5.14(C)**
A compare ballet and modern dance B show what Isadora Duncan looked like C compare the skills of male and female dancers **D show an example of modern dance**	

Warm-Up 9 • *Nature Girl*

Question & Answer	Standard
1 Which paragraph from Scene 1 supports the idea that Kaya is having trouble living in the city?	**5.5 Fig. 19(D)**
A ***KAYA: Grandma, I can't concentrate because the noise around here is so obnoxious! [She plops down on the couch.]***	
B *GRANDMA: [smiles in an inviting way] Well, this is New York—of course it's noisy outside.*	
C *ELI: Greetings, earthlings! Who wants Chinese food? [KAYA laughs and jumps up.]*	
D *[ELI, LEAH, KAYA, and GRANDMA start setting the table and opening containers.]*	
2 Which phrase from the selection gives a clue to the meaning of <u>skeptical</u> as it is used in paragraph 18?	**5.2(B)**
F *sacrificed herself to save others*	
G ***suspiciously inspecting every angle***	
H *fresh and nourishing—and yummy!*	
J *while the din of the city increases and the lights dim*	
3 Which line expresses a theme of the play?	**5.5 Fig. 19(D)**
A *Anyway, don't knock this kind of food until you try it. The Chinese food we get is excellent, and certainly better than succotash.*	
B *Corn Mother is part of an old tale from our Iroquois ancestors Do you know of the woman who gave her body to the earth to save her people?*	
C *Open your eyes and look carefully, and then tell me, what do you see?*	
D ***Just listen and look for the sounds of nature. Nature can nourish you and make you feel whole.***	
4 What inference can the reader make about Kaya and her family based on the dialogue in Scene 1?	**5.5 Fig. 19(D)**
F Kaya used to live in an Iroquois village before moving to the city.	
G **Grandma does not trust the food from restaurants.**	
H Kaya's parents and Grandma do not get along very well.	
J Grandma and Kaya met for the first time last year.	
5 Which line from the play suggests that Kaya and Leah don't always appreciate or relate to Grandma's views about her Iroquois heritage?	**5.5 Fig. 19(D)**
A *KAYA: Grandma, I can't concentrate because the noise around here is so obnoxious!*	
B *GRANDMA: [to LEAH] You know, I could have made dinner for everyone tonight.*	
C ***LEAH: Mom, please don't start.***	
D *KAYA: And the cars are canoes, and the streetlamps are lightning bugs!*	

Warm-Up 10 • Gordon Parks and His Camera

Question & Answer	Standard
1 In this selection, the author uses paragraphs 6 and 7 to – A introduce Gordon Parks's family to the reader B explain why Gordon Parks had trouble finding a job C show a less serious side of Gordon Parks **D explain how Gordon Parks got started as a photographer**	**5.7(A)**
2 In paragraph 8, the word <u>documenting</u> means – F trying to improve **G making a record of** H bringing about change in J analyzing the details of	**5.2(B)**
3 The author includes the two *American Gothic* photos in the selection to – A make readers want to see more of Parks's photos B identify an important person in Parks's life **C show the kind of work Parks did** D compare the skills of Gordon Parks and Grant Wood	**5.14(C)**
4 Which sentence from the selection explains how Gordon Parks chose many of the subjects for his photographs? **F *"I felt that I could somehow subdue these evils by doing something beautiful . . ."*** G *He spent years moving from place to place, struggling to earn enough to eat and have a place to live.* H *He worked as a fashion photographer in St Paul.* J *They worked hard on their small farm and taught their children strong religious values.*	**5.7(A)**
5 Which sentence from the selection supports the idea that Parks's photographs helped bring about changes in society and people's lives? A *The North wasn't strictly segregated by race, but throughout the country African Americans had few economic or educational opportunities.* B *He was so focused on the pictures that he fell into the ocean as he tried to photograph seagulls.* C *Then he moved to Chicago to do more fashion photography, but he also took his own pictures of people in the city.* **D *Some of his other photos persuaded American lawmakers to create programs to help people who were poor and hungry.***	**5.7 Fig. 19(D)**

Practice Test 1 • What Is a Satellite?

Question & Answer	Standard
1 What is this selection mainly about? A Scientists use satellites to study space because they can fly above the clouds. B Some satellites use energy from the sun to stay powered while orbiting Earth. C Earth and the moon are examples of natural satellites that orbit larger bodies. **D Satellites are used in many ways to help people communicate with each other and gather information.**	**5.11(A)**
2 Which sentence from the selection states a fact that can be verified? **F *A group of more than twenty satellites make up the Global Positioning System, or GPS.* **G *The bird's-eye view that satellites have allows them to see large areas of Earth at one time.* H *This ability means satellites can collect more data, more quickly, than instruments on the ground.* J *Satellites also can see into space better than telescopes on Earth's surface.*	**5.11(B)**
3 Based on the information in the selection, how do satellites help meteorologists? A by sending phone calls B by beaming TV signals **C by taking pictures of Earth** D by taking pictures of space	**5.11(A)**
4 Read this dictionary entry **launch** \lônch\ *verb* **1.** to put a boat or ship in the water **2.** to send forth or release **3.** to start a person on a course or career **4.** to start an application program on a computer Which definition best matches the word <u>launched</u> as it is used in paragraph 10? F Definition 1 **G Definition 2** H Definition 3 J Definition 4	**5.2(E)**
5 According to the selection, which of these is a use for satellites? A landing on and exploring other planets B getting rid of dust that blocks the view of Earth C changing the weather conditions in a given area **D helping GPS receivers figure out locations**	**5.11 Fig. 19(E)**

Question & Answer	Standard
6 In which section of the article should a reader look to find information about geostationary satellites? F the opening paragraphs G Why Are Satellites Important? H What Are the Parts of a Satellite? **J How Do Satellites Orbit Earth?**	**5.11(D)**
7 Which of these is a characteristic of both geostationary and polar-orbiting satellites? A They travel in a north-south direction. **B They are balanced by Earth's gravity.** C From Earth they appear to stand still. D They can scan the entire globe.	**5.11(E)**
8 In paragraph 4, why does the author compare the view of a satellite to that of a bird? F because birds can see at night G because birds have good eyesight **H because birds see the world from above** J because birds can see through large objects	**5.11 Fig. 19(E)**
9 What inference can the reader make based on the information in the section **Why Are Satellites Important?** A Satellites will soon replace all of the telescopes used by scientists. B Satellites have made it cheaper to send both TV signals and phone calls. C Satellites are much bigger now than they were when they were invented. **D Satellites have made it easier for people to communicate over long distances.**	**5.11 Fig. 19(D)**
10 By using comparison and contrast to organize the opening paragraphs in this selection, the author is able to — **F describe the differences between natural and artificial satellites** G explain how satellites stay in orbit around Earth H describe the events that took place in the development of satellites J explain how the parts of a satellite send and receive data	**5.11(C)**

Practice Test 2 • The Mill Girls of Lowell, Massachusetts

Question & Answer	Standard
1 Why did Francis Cabot Lowell visit the textile mills in England? **A to copy their machinery** B to see how mill workers lived C to write about the mills D to buy some of their textiles	**5.11(E)**
2 Which words from paragraph 6 help the reader understand the meaning of <u>confinement</u>? F *know that sometimes* G *very wearisome to me* **H *lean far out of the window*** J *the unceasing clash of sound*	**5.2(B)**
3 The author included an excerpt from Lucy Larcom's journal in this selection to – A entertain the reader with a humorous anecdote B give factual information about the Lowell mills C compare working in the mills with other jobs **D give a first-hand account of what the mills were like**	**5.10(A)**
4 What inference can the reader make about Lucy Larcom from the words she wrote, as quoted in this selection? F Lucy enjoyed working long hours, getting up early, and sticking to a schedule. **G When Lucy was young, the rigid mill schedule enforced by the bell caused her to feel defiant.** H Lucy came to believe that young people should not be permitted to dally and to dream. J Lucy was naturally inclined to choose a life of good discipline and regular habits.	**5.7 Fig. 19(D)**
5 The author includes a photo in this selection to – **A show what a Lowell factory workroom looked like** B describe the kind of cloth that was made in Lowell C show the work clothes that workers wore in the 1800s D describe the location of the Lowell mill buildings	**5.14(C)**
6 In paragraph 7, the word <u>torment</u> means – F fact of life G call to action H symbol of hope **J cause of suffering**	**5.2(B)**

Question & Answer	Standard
7 Both Lucy Larcom and Charles Dickens wrote about the lives of Lowell's mill girls. How were their points of view alike? A They both compared America with England. B They both worked in the mills. **C They both saw good qualities in Lowell mill workers' lives.** D They both told about negative features of mill work.	5.11(E)
8 Which detail from the selection supports the idea that many mill girls found opportunities to better themselves? F The workers had bells to tell them when to get up. **G Most of the workers belonged to circulating libraries.** H Many girls began working when they were eleven years old. J The girls lived in dormitories and boarding houses near the mill.	5.11 Fig. 19(D)
9 According to the selection, how did the mill owners make mill jobs attractive to young women? A They provided bonnets, warm cloaks, and shawls to all workers for free. B They paid the women extra to join a circulating library and write for a magazine. C They asked Charles Dickens to explain that mills in England were much worse. **D They offered higher pay than most jobs and safe, clean places to live.**	5.11(A)
10 Which of these is the best summary of the article? F In 1814, Boston Associates built America's first textile mill in Waltham, Massachusetts. Soon afterward, the company built a whole city called Lowell with textile mills powered by water. Girls from farms in the surrounding area worked in the mills. **G Francis Cabot Lowell and his associates built America's first successful textile mill in Massachusetts in the early 1800s. They hired young women to work in the mills. The mill girls worked long hours but still found time for education and the arts.** H When Francis Cabot Lowell built a textile mill in the early 1800s, Lucy Larcom got a job there. She worked long hours and found the work difficult, but she enjoyed the money and found other ways to improve herself. J Francis Cabot Lowell went to England in the early 1800s to see the English textile mills. The Industrial Age had already begun in England, and Lowell brought industry to America. He hired many young women to work in his factory.	5.11 Fig. 19(E)

 STAAR Reading Warm-Ups & Test Practice Grade 5 • ©2014 Newmark Learning, LLC

Practice Test 3 • Curry Without Shortcuts • The Real Princess

Question & Answer	Standard
1 Which phrase from "Curry Without Shortcuts" helps the reader understand the meaning of <u>fragrant</u> in paragraph 15? A *measuring out coriander and cumin* **B *aroma of spices*** C *feared that she might not like it* D *strange and new*	**5.2(B)**
2 In "Curry Without Shortcuts," the narrator tells the story from the point of view of — **F Julie** G Julie's mother H Priya J Priya's mother	**5.6(C)**
3 In "Curry Without Shortcuts," how do Julie and her mother feel after making their first curry dish? A pleased B excited C resentful **D discouraged**	**5.6 Fig. 19(D)**
4 How do the two cooking scenes in "Curry Without Shortcuts" fit together to provide the structure to the story? F They provide a comparison of two characters in the story. **G They provide a contrast that helps develop the theme of the story.** H They show two steps leading to the solution of the conflict in the story. J They tell the cause of a problem and its effect on the characters in the story.	**5.6(A)**
5 What happens as a result of Priya's invitation in "Curry Without Shortcuts"? A Julie and her mother decide to make the curry with substituted ingredients. B Julie asks her mother for help making a new recipe for curry. **C Julie enjoys a curry dinner and realizes the importance of following a recipe.** D Julie forgets to bring the leftover curry home and her mother gets upset.	**5.6(B)**

Question & Answer	Standard
6 In paragraph 15 of "Curry Without Shortcuts," the word <u>intimidating</u> comes from a Latin root that means – F very tasty G dull or boring H having strength **J causing fear**	**5.2(A)**
7 How can the reader tell that "The Real Princess" is a fairy tale? **A It involves a prince and princess who do not have names.** B It tells the story of a man who wants to find a wife. C The events of the story took place a long time ago. D The main character's mother gets involved in the events.	**5.3 Fig. 19(D)**
8 Based on the story "The Real Princess," what inference can the reader make about the Prince? F The Prince does not like many people that he meets. G The Prince is clever and can find ways to tell if a woman is a real Princess. **H The Prince believes that a real Princess has qualities that make her different from other women.** J The Prince would be able to feel the three peas through the twenty mattresses.	**5.6 Fig. 19(D)**
9 How would "The Real Princess" be different if it were told from the point of view of the Princess? A The story would include more details about what the bed looked like. B The story would include the thoughts of all of the characters. C The story would include more details about the castle. **D The story would include the thoughts of the Princess.**	**5.6(C)**
10 In "The Real Princess," what is the meaning of <u>tempest</u> as it is used in paragraph 2? F blackout G flood H nighttime **J storm**	**5.2(B)**

Question & Answer	Standard
11 How is the Queen-mother different from the other characters in "The Real Princess"? A She does not trust other people. **B She takes action to find the truth.** C She thinks she is better than other people. D She does not want her son to get married.	**5.3 Fig. 19(D)**
12 In what way are the Queen-mother in "The Real Princess" and Priya in "Curry Without Shortcuts" alike? **F They both help solve a problem.** G They both are suspicious of strangers. H They both spend a lot of time with their families. J They both are happy when their plan is successful.	**5.19(F)**
13 What lesson can be learned from both of these stories? A Princesses look and act differently from other women. B It can be frightening sometimes to try new things. C Curry and other foods never taste as good as they should. **D It is worth the time and effort to do things right.**	**5.3(A)**
14 In "The Real Princess," which sentence does the author use to add playful humor to the story? F *He traveled all over the world in hopes of finding such a lady; but there was always something wrong.* G *All at once there was heard a violent knocking at the door, and the old King, the Prince's father, went out himself to open it.* H *The Prince accordingly made her his wife; being now convinced that he had found a real Princess.* **J *The three peas were however put into the cabinet of curiosities, where they are still to be seen, provided they are not lost.***	**5.8(A)**
15 "The Real Princess" is mostly about a Prince who – A likes to invent challenging tests that people cannot pass **B thinks he can only be happy with a certain kind of wife** C enjoys traveling and does not wish to settle down D hopes to marry a woman who is just like his mother	**5.3 Fig. 19(E)**

Practice Test 4 • The Berlin Wall • Tear Down This Wall!

Question & Answer	Standard
1 In paragraph 4 of "The Berlin Wall," the word <u>unified</u> comes from a Latin root that means — A conquered B ruled **C made into one** D freed from prison	**5.2(A)**
2 Which sentence from "The Berlin Wall" supports the idea that the Soviet Union wanted to stop people from leaving East Germany? F *Instead, they woke up to find that the streets connecting the two sides of the city had been torn up.* **G *For twenty-eight years, the only way the people of East Germany could reach West Berlin was by attempting to escape across the wall.*** H *Germany functioned as a single country for more than seventy years.* J *Germany was in the center of the two great World Wars in the twentieth century.*	**5.11(E)**
3 How does the author of "The Berlin Wall" support the point that there were many reasons why people in East Germany wanted to move to West Germany? A By describing details of daily life in East and West Germany **B By contrasting the jobs and freedoms in East and West Germany** C By comparing life before and after East and West Germany were separated D By stating where people could go once they left East Germany for West Germany	**5.11(C)**
4 According to "The Berlin Wall," why did the victors of World War II divide Germany in half? F They wanted Germany to be separated like Berlin. G They wanted part of Germany to be just like the Soviet Union. **H They wanted to stop Germany from becoming powerful again.** J They wanted to return Germany to the way it was before World War I.	**5.11(A)**
5 Which sentence from "The Berlin Wall" states a fact that can be verified? A *East Berlin had become a prison.* B *Its people worked hard at well-paying jobs.* C *They could travel where they wanted and vote in free elections.* **D *By 1961, 2.5 million people had fled East Germany.***	**5.11(B)**

Question & Answer	Standard
6 Read this dictionary entry **major** \mājər\ *noun* **1.** a military officer above a captain **2.** a field of study or subject that a student specializes in *adjective* **3.** of great importance **4.** of great risk; serious Which definition best matches the word <u>major</u> as it is used in paragraph 1 of "Tear Down This Wall!"? F Definition 1 G Definition 2 **H Definition 3** J Definition 4	**5.2(E)**
7 According to "Tear Down This Wall!" why were the peace talks between Reagan and Gorbachev "historic"? A They happened many years ago. **B They helped bring about great change in the world.** C They took place between the United States and the Soviet Union. D They continued the work Reagan had begun as governor of California.	**5.12(A)**
8 Which sentence should be included in a summary of "Tear Down This Wall!"? F The Berlin Wall was built at the end of World War II. G Reagan and Gorbachev met several times between 1985 and 1988. **H During a trip to Berlin, Reagan asked Gorbachev to tear down the Berlin Wall.** J Reagan's achievements made him a great president.	**5.12 Fig. 19(E)**
9 According to "The Berlin Wall," why did East Germans want to escape to West Germany? A They wanted to follow their religious beliefs. B They wanted to fly to the United States. C They wanted to show support for President Reagan. **D They wanted freedom and economic opportunity.**	**5.11(A)**
10 What was President Reagan's main point in his "Tear Down This Wall!" speech? **F Freedom leads to economic success.** G Nothing is as important as world peace. H Foreign news broadcasts are important. J People in the West have false hopes.	**5.12(A)**

Question & Answer	Standard
11 Which detail from Reagan's speech in "Tear Down This Wall!" uses exaggeration to make a point? A *. . . in the West today, we see a free world* **B *In the Communist world, we see failure, technological backwardness. . .*** C *. . . coming to understand the importance of freedom* D *There is one sign the Soviets can make that would be unmistakable. . .*	**5.12(B)**
12 What inference can be made about the author's opinion of Ronald Reagan in "Tear Down This Wall!"? F The author likes Reagan but did not like the speech he made. **G The author admires Reagan and thinks he did an important thing.** H The author dislikes Reagan and believes his speech was a huge mistake. J The author does not think Reagan understood the Soviet government.	**5.12(A)**
13 In both "The Berlin Wall" and "Tear Down This Wall!" the authors organize and present information mainly by — A explaining events in order of their importance **B telling what happened in chronological order** C asking questions and giving the answers D describing a problem and its solution	**5.19(F)**
14 What is the main focus in both of these selections? F the Soviet Union G President Reagan **H the Berlin Wall** J East Germany	**5.19(F)**
15 The author includes a photo in "The Berlin Wall" to — **A show what the wall looked like** B prove that a wall was built C compare East and West Berlin D show the soldiers of East Germany	**5.14(C)**

Practice Test 5 • from *The Call of the Wild* • Thor's Hammer

Question & Answer	Standard
1 In the selection from *The Call of the Wild*, what is the meaning of the word <u>treachery</u> as it is used in paragraph 2? A loss of faith B escape from a place C agreement **D act of betrayal**	**5.2(B)**
2 Based on this selection, what event in history provided a reason for this story? **F Gold was discovered in the Klondike.** G Settlers moved west to California. H The War Between the States began. J The United States signed a treaty with Canada.	**5.3(C)**
3 Why did Manuel kidnap Buck? A Buck was mean and could not be tamed. **B He planned to sell Buck as a sled dog.** C The Judge wanted to get rid of Buck. D He was afraid Buck would bite him.	**5.3(C)**
4 In the selection from *The Call of the Wild*, which sentence shows that the man who takes Buck to San Francisco regrets what he has done? F *"Yep, has fits," the man said, hiding his mangled hand from the baggageman, who had been attracted by the sounds of struggle.* G *Concerning that night's ride, the man spoke most eloquently for himself, in a little shed back of a saloon on the San Francisco water front.* **H** *"All I get is fifty for it," he grumbled; "an' I wouldn't do it over for a thousand, cold cash."* J *His hand was wrapped in a bloody handkerchief, and the right trouser leg was ripped from knee to ankle.*	**5.6 Fig. 19(D)**

Question & Answer	Standard
5 How does the narrative point of view in this selection from *The Call of the Wild* affect the reader's experience with the story? A The reader knows how the men look and act but not what happens to the dog. **B The reader learns how Buck feels and thinks, and how he reacts to each event.** C The reader experiences the story from Manuel's point of view. D The reader relates to the men more closely than to the dog.	**5.6(C)**
6 What can the reader infer from the illustration in the selection from *The Call of the Wild*? F The train car Buck rode in was cold and dark. G Buck was not strong enough to pull a dog sled. H The man who took Buck could not control him. **J Buck was mistreated by the men who took him.**	**5.14(C)**
7 Which sentence from *The Call of the Wild* helps the reader understand how Buck feels about the way he is treated? **A *Then the rope tightened mercilessly, while Buck struggled in a fury, his tongue lolling out of his mouth and his great chest panting futilely.*** B *But his strength ebbed, his eyes glazed, and he knew nothing when the train was flagged and the two men threw him into the baggage car.* C *He had travelled too often with the Judge not to know the sensation of riding in a baggage car.* D *Then the rope was removed, and he was flung into a cagelike crate.*	**5.6(B)**
8 Which of these is the best summary of the selection from *The Call of the Wild*? F Judge Miller went to a meeting one night. A man named Manuel worked for Judge Miller. Manuel took Judge Miller's dog for a walk. G Manuel worked in California on an estate. He had a dog named Buck. When Manuel decided to go to Canada to mine for gold, he took Buck with him on the train. **H A dog named Buck was taken from Judge Miller's estate. Buck was sold, put into a cage, and loaded onto a train. A man tried to control the dog, but Buck fought hard.** J Manuel and Buck took a walk to the train station. A man with a rope and a club attacked them and kidnapped the dog. The man put Buck in a cage on a train.	**5.6 Fig. 19(E)**

   STAAR Reading Warm-Ups & Test Practice Grade 5 • ©2014 Newmark Learning, LLC

Question & Answer	Standard
9 In "Thor's Hammer," which phrase helps the reader understand the meaning of <u>ravenous</u> in paragraph 18? A *nervous anticipation that makes Freya quiver* B *swept the gnawed bones from the table* C *called a servant to bring more food* **D *could not eat for eight days***	**5.2(B)**
10 According to the selection, Thor and his hammer created what natural phenomenon? F mountains G frost **H thunder** J oxen	**5.3(B)**
11 In "Thor's Hammer," why do the gods hide their laughter as Thor and Loki depart for the land of the Frost Giants? A They played a trick on Thor. B They do not want to hurt Thor's feelings. C They think Thor will refuse to go. **D They are afraid of Thor's wrath.**	**5.3 Fig. 19(D)**
12 In "Thor's Hammer," why doesn't Thrym realize that his "bride" is actually Thor disguised as Freya? F He does not get close enough to have a good look at Thor. **G He believes the excuses Loki offers to his questions.** H He does not want to seem foolish in front of the other Frost Giants. J The lighting in the banquet hall is too dim to see Thor.	**5.3 Fig. 19(D)**

Question & Answer	Standard
13 In paragraph 19 of "Thor's Hammer," the author compares Thor's eyes to "fiery red coals" to – A make Thor seem attractive B emphasize Loki's cleverness C explain why Thrym was fooled **D show how angry Thor was**	**5.8(A)**
14 In "Thor's Hammer," how does the narrator's point of view influence the story? F The narrator makes the reader feel afraid of Thor. G The narrator seems to suggest that people who believe in myths are foolish. H The narrator makes Thor seem heroic by favoring him over the other gods. **J The narrator presents the tale as if the gods and goddesses are real.**	**5.3(B)**
15 In "Thor's Hammer," the author includes an illustration to – A show how strong Thor is B compare Thor and the trickster Loki **C show what Thor looks like in disguise** D suggest that Thor really does look like Freya	**5.14(C)**

Answer Forms

Answer Form • Practice Test 1

Name_______________________________________ Date___________

1 Ⓐ Ⓑ Ⓒ Ⓓ

2 Ⓕ Ⓖ Ⓗ Ⓙ

3 Ⓐ Ⓑ Ⓒ Ⓓ

4 Ⓕ Ⓖ Ⓗ Ⓙ

5 Ⓐ Ⓑ Ⓒ Ⓓ

6 Ⓕ Ⓖ Ⓗ Ⓙ

7 Ⓐ Ⓑ Ⓒ Ⓓ

8 Ⓕ Ⓖ Ⓗ Ⓙ

9 Ⓐ Ⓑ Ⓒ Ⓓ

10 Ⓕ Ⓖ Ⓗ Ⓙ

Answer Form • Practice Test 2

Name______________________________ Date__________

1 Ⓐ Ⓑ Ⓒ Ⓓ

2 Ⓕ Ⓖ Ⓗ Ⓙ

3 Ⓐ Ⓑ Ⓒ Ⓓ

4 Ⓕ Ⓖ Ⓗ Ⓙ

5 Ⓐ Ⓑ Ⓒ Ⓓ

6 Ⓕ Ⓖ Ⓗ Ⓙ

7 Ⓐ Ⓑ Ⓒ Ⓓ

8 Ⓕ Ⓖ Ⓗ Ⓙ

9 Ⓐ Ⓑ Ⓒ Ⓓ

10 Ⓕ Ⓖ Ⓗ Ⓙ

Answer Form • Practice Test 3

Name________________________________ Date__________

1 Ⓐ Ⓑ Ⓒ Ⓓ

2 Ⓕ Ⓖ Ⓗ Ⓙ

3 Ⓐ Ⓑ Ⓒ Ⓓ

4 Ⓕ Ⓖ Ⓗ Ⓙ

5 Ⓐ Ⓑ Ⓒ Ⓓ

6 Ⓕ Ⓖ Ⓗ Ⓙ

7 Ⓐ Ⓑ Ⓒ Ⓓ

8 Ⓕ Ⓖ Ⓗ Ⓙ

9 Ⓐ Ⓑ Ⓒ Ⓓ

10 Ⓕ Ⓖ Ⓗ Ⓙ

11 Ⓐ Ⓑ Ⓒ Ⓓ

12 Ⓕ Ⓖ Ⓗ Ⓙ

13 Ⓐ Ⓑ Ⓒ Ⓓ

14 Ⓕ Ⓖ Ⓗ Ⓙ

15 Ⓐ Ⓑ Ⓒ Ⓓ

Name_____ Date_____

1 Ⓐ Ⓑ Ⓒ Ⓓ   11 Ⓐ Ⓑ Ⓒ Ⓓ

2 Ⓕ Ⓖ Ⓗ Ⓙ   12 Ⓕ Ⓖ Ⓗ Ⓙ

3 Ⓐ Ⓑ Ⓒ Ⓓ   13 Ⓐ Ⓑ Ⓒ Ⓓ

4 Ⓕ Ⓖ Ⓗ Ⓙ   14 Ⓕ Ⓖ Ⓗ Ⓙ

5 Ⓐ Ⓑ Ⓒ Ⓓ   15 Ⓐ Ⓑ Ⓒ Ⓓ

6 Ⓕ Ⓖ Ⓗ Ⓙ

7 Ⓐ Ⓑ Ⓒ Ⓓ

8 Ⓕ Ⓖ Ⓗ Ⓙ

9 Ⓐ Ⓑ Ⓒ Ⓓ

10 Ⓕ Ⓖ Ⓗ Ⓙ

Name_____ Date_____

1 Ⓐ Ⓑ Ⓒ Ⓓ   11 Ⓐ Ⓑ Ⓒ Ⓓ

2 Ⓕ Ⓖ Ⓗ Ⓙ   12 Ⓕ Ⓖ Ⓗ Ⓙ

3 Ⓐ Ⓑ Ⓒ Ⓓ   13 Ⓐ Ⓑ Ⓒ Ⓓ

4 Ⓕ Ⓖ Ⓗ Ⓙ   14 Ⓕ Ⓖ Ⓗ Ⓙ

5 Ⓐ Ⓑ Ⓒ Ⓓ   15 Ⓐ Ⓑ Ⓒ Ⓓ

6 Ⓕ Ⓖ Ⓗ Ⓙ

7 Ⓐ Ⓑ Ⓒ Ⓓ

8 Ⓕ Ⓖ Ⓗ Ⓙ

9 Ⓐ Ⓑ Ⓒ Ⓓ

10 Ⓕ Ⓖ Ⓗ Ⓙ

Name_____ Date_____

1 Ⓐ Ⓑ Ⓒ Ⓓ	1 Ⓐ Ⓑ Ⓒ Ⓓ	1 Ⓐ Ⓑ Ⓒ Ⓓ
2 Ⓕ Ⓖ Ⓗ Ⓙ	2 Ⓕ Ⓖ Ⓗ Ⓙ	2 Ⓕ Ⓖ Ⓗ Ⓙ
3 Ⓐ Ⓑ Ⓒ Ⓓ	3 Ⓐ Ⓑ Ⓒ Ⓓ	3 Ⓐ Ⓑ Ⓒ Ⓓ
4 Ⓕ Ⓖ Ⓗ Ⓙ	4 Ⓕ Ⓖ Ⓗ Ⓙ	4 Ⓕ Ⓖ Ⓗ Ⓙ
5 Ⓐ Ⓑ Ⓒ Ⓓ	5 Ⓐ Ⓑ Ⓒ Ⓓ	5 Ⓐ Ⓑ Ⓒ Ⓓ
6 Ⓕ Ⓖ Ⓗ Ⓙ	6 Ⓕ Ⓖ Ⓗ Ⓙ	6 Ⓕ Ⓖ Ⓗ Ⓙ
7 Ⓐ Ⓑ Ⓒ Ⓓ	7 Ⓐ Ⓑ Ⓒ Ⓓ	7 Ⓐ Ⓑ Ⓒ Ⓓ
8 Ⓕ Ⓖ Ⓗ Ⓙ	8 Ⓕ Ⓖ Ⓗ Ⓙ	8 Ⓕ Ⓖ Ⓗ Ⓙ
9 Ⓐ Ⓑ Ⓒ Ⓓ	9 Ⓐ Ⓑ Ⓒ Ⓓ	9 Ⓐ Ⓑ Ⓒ Ⓓ
10 Ⓕ Ⓖ Ⓗ Ⓙ	10 Ⓕ Ⓖ Ⓗ Ⓙ	10 Ⓕ Ⓖ Ⓗ Ⓙ
	11 Ⓐ Ⓑ Ⓒ Ⓓ	11 Ⓐ Ⓑ Ⓒ Ⓓ
	12 Ⓕ Ⓖ Ⓗ Ⓙ	12 Ⓕ Ⓖ Ⓗ Ⓙ
	13 Ⓐ Ⓑ Ⓒ Ⓓ	13 Ⓐ Ⓑ Ⓒ Ⓓ
	14 Ⓕ Ⓖ Ⓗ Ⓙ	14 Ⓕ Ⓖ Ⓗ Ⓙ
	15 Ⓐ Ⓑ Ⓒ Ⓓ	15 Ⓐ Ⓑ Ⓒ Ⓓ

Notes